FORGOTTEN TEARS

A Grandmother's Journey Through Grief

FORGOTTEN TEARS

A Grandmother's Journey Through Grief

by

Nina Bennett

Give sorrow words
The grief that does not speak
Whispers the o'er fraught heart
And bids it break

William Shakespeare
Macbeth

In Memory Of

Maddy Hodgdon

My precious granddaughter

and

My beloved sister, Blair Bennett, who loved her nephew, Tim,
and would have adored and spoiled her great-niece

Acknowledgements

I am blessed to have very special people in my life. Without their support, encouragement and love during my grief journey this book would not be possible. I truly wish there had been no need for me to write it. I would like to acknowledge and thank:

Michele Delmonico for her unconditional love and support over all the years, her patience in listening to my story over and over-when it comes to girlfriends, I sure know how to pick them!

Mark Manchen for his vigilant friendship, hugs, phone calls and e-mails. You took my hand and showed me I could dance again.

Pat Lincoln and Mary Ann Bartkowski for providing a safe place and allowing me to grieve on my own time line.

Br. Kevin O'Loughlin for his daily e- mails, prayers and concern for my spirit. You were my faith when I felt as though I had none.

From the very bottom of my heart, I thank the entire staff of the Birth Center, especially Peggy, Marissa, and Dorinda. Although I am jealous that you knew Maddy far better than I did, I am eternally grateful to you for the love and warmth you showed Jenn, Tim, and Maddy. You are unique women, and you belong exactly where you are. May Maddy's life and death reinforce your commitment to providing personal, holistic, loving care to women and their families.

I have a love and appreciation for the following family members that can never be adequately expressed. Thank you doesn't begin to convey how I feel.

Benjamin and Tiffany Hodgdon, for their caring and constant devotion to Tim and Jenn.

Brandon and Kristyn Hodgdon, for providing me with happiness, joy and a never ending supply of hugs and kisses.

Jim and Hilda Bennett, for showing us all that it is possible to survive the death of a child.

Brian Bennett, who has been my travel companion through so many journeys of every kind imaginable.

Timothy and Jennifer Hodgdon, who from the moment I first mentioned the idea, had a steadfast belief that this book would indeed be written. How they were able to support and encourage me through their pain is yet one more testament to their courage and strength.

Maddy's Grandfathers, Bill Skahan and Dick Hodgdon-may you find peace.

No book about Maddy could be written without a special acknowledgement to her maternal Great Grandmother, Madeline, for whom she was named, and on whose birthday, November 12, she was born still.

Forgotten Tears is dedicated to Kathy Skahan, Maddy's maternal Grandmother, whose tears became my words.

Strangers in Life, Sisters in Grief

In my frantic search for information on the internet, I discovered three organizations with online support groups specifically for grandparents. Talking about Maddy and my feelings and experiences was immensely helpful, and I definitely recommend these groups, as only another grandparent who has suffered the death of a grandchild truly understands the many facets of grief experienced by grandparents. I have developed a very close friendship with one of the women, Wilma Whitman, who used the phrase strangers in life, sisters in grief in one of her many moving e-mails to me. Wilma's grandson Jackson was stillborn on the same day as my granddaughter; this was the first of many so-called coincidences that are discussed throughout this book. I feel a very powerful connection to Wilma, and I have a feeling we won't remain strangers. During my search for other grandparents willing to share their grief journey, I have been blessed to have two more grandmothers enter my life. Beryle Greenwald's grandson Dakota was stillborn in 1999. One of the ways Beryle honors her grandson is by counseling other bereaved grandparents. Through Beryle, I was introduced to Margo Einsig, whose grandson Peyton was stillborn a few months before Maddy. Although I would never have wished for any grandparent to be making this journey, I am grateful for the company of these remarkable women. Their frequent words of support, encouragement, understanding and love have enabled me to endure the unendurable. It is an honor to call them sisters. These women are quoted frequently throughout the book. I thank them for being willing to share their thoughts and feelings and experiences so openly. Maddy, Jackson, Peyton and Kota are surely romping through the stars together.

A very grateful thanks to Donnali Fifield for her selfless guidance and encouragement. Her input and suggestions helped to focus and direct my writing.

I also need to give thanks to another very special woman in my life-my mother. Hilda Bennett has survived not one but two of the most horrendous tragedies life has to offer. She has watched the coffin of the second child she gave life to be lowered into the ground. She emerged from the despair of my sister's death with an even firmer belief in the importance of family, a belief she has steadfastly instilled in her children and grandchildren. She pulls her family around her like a quilt, drawing comfort and love and happiness from each of us, and returning it many times over. She has a warm and special relationship with her great grandchildren, and spends a great deal of time with them. At a time when she was so excited at the prospect of her youngest grandson's first child, she had to receive the news that the eagerly awaited baby had not survived delivery. Her grief has been layered on top of seeing her daughter and grandson in pain. Any strength I have has come from this incredible woman. I can only hope to one day become the remarkable person she is. I love you, Mom.

Permissions

I would like to acknowledge the following people, who gave me permission to quote from their articles, books, and/or web site, all of which are listed in the bibliography. I also wish to thank the people who assisted me by posting my request for grandparents to share their journey on web sites, discussion forums, and in newsletters. Even more important, I want them to know how grateful I am for their encouragement during the writing of this book. I am deeply appreciative of the many personal messages of empathy. These are the Hansels and Gretels of my grief journey, the people who lined my path with their own pain and insight, to show me the way.

Lorraine Ash *Life Touches Life*

Association for Death Education and Counseling (ADEC) Tom Easthope,CDE, *Nipped in the Bud;* Mary Lou Reed,RN, MA, *Grandparents' Grief-Who is Listening?*

Joanne Cacciatore-Garard, Executive Director of MISS Foundation, *Wonderment*

Margo Einsig *Letter to Peyton*

Donnali Fifield *William & Wendell: A Family Remembered*

Kathleen Gilbert, PhD., C.F.L.E., CT, *Grief in a Family Context*

Tom Golden, LCSW, *Swallowed by the Snake: The Gift of the Masculine Side of Healing*

Susan Hendricks *Katrina*

Sandy Hoffman *Grandparent's Grief Does Not Care How*

Kara Jones kotapress.com

Paula Long honoredbabies.org

The Compassionate Friends national office Nancy Moyer, *New Year's Resolutions for Bereaved Grandparents*

Marty Tousley, RN, MS, CS, CT, *Getting Through the Holidays*

Lee Ward AGAST agast.org Margaret Gerner, *Grief of Grandparents*

Alan Wolfelt, PhD. *Why is the Funeral Ritual Important? Helping Yourself Heal When Someone Dies. Helping Yourself Heal When Your Child Dies*

My heart overflows with gratitude for the grandparents who responded and agreed to share their grief journey. I cry your tears, as you cry mine. Thank you for reaching through your grief to share your love for your child and grandchild. That enduring love is evident in every e-mail, letter and phone call. Together, we can ensure that our grandchildren as well as our tears will never be forgotten.

John and Cheryl Cox, grandparents of A.J.
Carla Earnhardt, grandmother of Braxton
Margo Einsig, grandmother of Peyton
Pat Fife, grandmother of Bridgid
Nancy B. Fuller, grandmother of Ethan
Beryle Greenwald, grandmother of Dakota
Mary Lou Reed, grandmother of Alex
Sharon Stepleton, grandmother of Paige
Wilma Whitman, grandmother of Jackson

TABLE OF CONTENTS

INTRODUCTION

I am only one; but still I am one. I cannot do everything, but still I can do something; I will not refuse to do the something I can do.

Helen Keller

"She doesn't have a heartbeat." My entire life changed in the time it took for my son to utter those five words. As I've struggled to make sense of the events surrounding my granddaughter's stillbirth, I've discovered that there is little written about the impact of infant death on grandparents. There is a great deal of information available on grief and bereavement in general. There is, fortunately, a large selection of written information on pregnancy loss, primarily written to assist parents in coping. There are even resources for helping children deal with the death of a sibling. Grandparents are usually given a page or two in a book. We don't even rate an entire chapter. I work for the oldest and largest hospital system in my state, and the bereavement leave granted for a grandchild's death is one day. It's as though the bond and love and despair that we feel shouldn't exist.

I have an extensive professional and personal background dealing with issues of death and bereavement. I served on the Board of Directors of my local Childbirth Education Association and taught prepared childbirth classes for many years, and dealt with issues of pregnancy loss. I've been working in the HIV/AIDS field since the beginning of the epidemic. I have personally attended more deaths than I care to count. I have provided bereavement counseling for partners and family members. I've taught workshops on bereavement to professionals working in the HIV field.

I also, unfortunately, have experienced the death of a sibling. My sister died quite unexpectedly at the age of thirty-two. She was living across the country from our family, so there were numerous frantic and complicated travel preparations involved. She was in a trauma center on life support, and she lived for exactly one week. During that time I assumed the role of the strong and knowledgeable family member, consulting with the medical staff frequently, interpreting changes in her status for my parents and brother, and stroking her and holding her as she died. I believed that my strength was defined by the fact that I didn't cry. After the funeral, many people remarked about how organized and calm I was. I felt a sense of pride when I overheard relatives and friends comment on how lucky my parents were to have me nearby to take care of them through this ordeal. These words reinforced the image of the stoic face that I presented in public. It wasn't until years later, as I studied death and grief on a professional level, that I even began to think about the fact that I had never been given a chance to openly mourn my sister. All of my grieving had been done in private. People asked me often how my mother was doing, infrequently somebody asked after my father, but never did anybody comfort me for my loss of a sibling. Psychologists say that every loss is compounded by past losses, especially ones that aren't fully mourned.

None of this professional and life experience prepared me for the onslaught of emotions when my granddaughter died. My usual reaction to anything is to research and read everything I can find. As I searched the internet, going to web site after web site, reading book after book on pregnancy loss and bereavement, I found myself becoming resentful. Where was the information on grandparents? Where were the interviews with the men and women who were so eagerly anticipating this wonderful new phase of their lives? Where were the coping skills and resources for those of us who not only are grieving ourselves, but feeling absolutely powerless to alleviate our son or daughter's suffering?

In searching for some way to incorporate this event into my being, and to give lasting meaning to Maddy's life, I decided to write this book, using my journal entries as a starting point. I have dreamed of writing a book my entire life; this is the one book I never imagined I would write. One of the many gifts my granddaughter has given me is the impetus and discipline to write. I will try not to let her down. I will tell her story, I will bear public witness to her life and the place she holds in mine, and hopefully, along the way, other grandparents will also find some peace.

The intention of this book is not to provide in depth medical information regarding the death of a baby. It is, rather, a book about the grief journey, specifically my grief journey. While it does contain very personal thoughts and feelings, I've attempted to explore the broader issues faced by grandparents, and to offer suggestions based on numerous discussions with other bereaved grandparents. Originally, I wrote from a general point of view, attempting to summarize my journal entries. As I reread sections I had written, I felt as though much of it sounded clinical, as though I was observing myself. That is, indeed, how I felt in those first weeks-as though I was watching from a distance. I realized that the only way to accurately portray what I was experiencing was to quote directly from my journal. I am, by nature, a very private person. I tend to keep things inside. The decision to share my journal entries was a difficult one. Many of the details may be as painful to read as they were to write. My goal is not to produce a pessimistic viewpoint, but rather to provide some insight into the complexity of the grieving process, and to help other grandparents realize that they are not alone. Friends and colleagues of grandparents who have experienced the death of a grandchild will be better able to understand how this event has affected and transformed us.

I want to clarify my use of the words birth and death. When referring to my granddaughter, because her birth and death were virtually simultaneous, I use the words interchangeably. Her situation was unusual in that she did not die prior to labor beginning. There was no indication of fetal distress during labor. Our best guess is that she died during delivery.

Although this book is written from the point of view of a grandmother, I am hoping that parents experiencing the death of a baby will read it also. Perhaps it will help them to realize how many people love their baby, and how intensely grandparents grieve. Ideally, parents and their adult children will be drawn closer by sharing a powerful bond-not just the bond of mourning the death, but the bond of acknowledging the love, hopes and dreams that resulted from the anticipation of the baby. At the very least, I need to register another voice asking that the experience of stillbirth be examined and openly discussed, thus giving parents, grandparents and other family members a safe, welcoming environment in which to grieve.

CHAPTER 1

BABIES AREN'T SUPPOSED TO DIE

*Well has it been said that there is no grief like the grief which does
not speak*
Henry Wadsworth Longfellow

It isn't fair. Babies aren't supposed to die, especially in this age of medical miracles. When a baby dies, it defies the natural order of things. We are not supposed to outlive our children or our grandchildren. It just isn't right. From my years working in prenatal and reproductive health, I was certainly aware pregnancies don't always produce a healthy baby. I was familiar with the statistics for miscarriage-approximately 15-20% of known pregnancies end before the twentieth week. I was aware of the possibility of a baby being born prematurely or with conditions incompatible with continued life. I had some experience with stillbirth, which is defined as a pregnancy beyond twenty weeks gestation resulting in the delivery of a dead baby, but I had no idea what the actual statistics were until I started looking for information. The statistics on stillbirth are not exact because there are no standardized guidelines for reporting and investigating stillbirths. Some states don't require fetal death certificates. Fetal autopsy rates are low. According to the March of Dimes, stillbirth occurs in about 1 in 200 pregnancies. Each year in the United States more than 26,000 babies are stillborn. Simply put, 71 babies are stillborn in this country every single day. 142 mothers and fathers return with empty arms to a home filled with shattered dreams. 568 grandparents are devastated on a daily basis, feeling isolated in their own grief and powerless to help their children. The medical care providers are left shaken and mourning as well. Up to half of all stillbirths occur in pregnancies that had seemed problem free, and about 14% of these deaths occur during labor and delivery. The International Stillbirth Alliance reports that "unexplained stillbirth in late pregnancy is the single largest cause of death in perinatal life in the Western world." The National Institute of Child Health and Human Development (NICHD), which is one of the National Institutes of Health (NIH), announced on November 19 2003 that they had awarded funding for the Stillbirth Research Collaborative Network. This is a five-year national research effort to study stillbirth in the United States. In the press release announcing this initiative, NICHD states that the number of reported deaths from stillbirth is equal to that of all infant deaths combined. "The purpose of the study is to understand the scope of the problem, and then to understand what causes stillbirth," says Dr. Catherine Spong, chief of the pregnancy and perinatology branch of the NICHD.

We feel a need to make sense of major traumatic events. There is absolutely no sense to be made of a baby dying. Many parents decide not to have their baby autopsied. Knowing what caused the baby's death doesn't always answer the question as to why. Even if an autopsy is performed, between one-third and one-half of the time a definitive cause of death is not established. If this is the case, it is extremely hard for parents and grandparents to accept that they will never know exactly what went wrong. Being able to resolve and accept is a major step in the traditional grief process. We are expected to accept not only that the baby has died, but also the fact that this does not and never will make sense.

As the numbness started to wear off, these were the thoughts going through my head. Maddy never had a chance. She never drew a breath. The unjustness of this threatened to overwhelm me. The death of a baby affects everyone. My friends and co-workers were nearly as stunned and saddened as I was. Their understanding of the magnitude of my loss was a source of support for me in the weeks and months that followed Maddy's death.

Our society does not do a good job of dealing with death. We are uncomfortable discussing the subject. We don't know what to say to someone who has experienced a death in the family. We put off calling them or avoid seeing them because we just don't know what to say or do. When it is a baby that has died, this uncomfortable reaction is heightened. People are reluctant to talk about the baby because they mistakenly believe it will make things worse for the grieving family. How could anybody possibly make this worse? What actually makes things worse is thinking that nobody cares about our loss. We need to know that others realize what an impact this loss has had on us. Several friends told me "I don't know what to say" or "What can I possibly say?" To me, this was the most sincere condolence offered. I didn't want to hear the cliches about time healing. I wanted people to acknowledge and validate the enormity of my loss.

This general reluctance and discomfort discussing death plays itself out in the prenatal field. Medical professionals, when providing prenatal care, do not discuss the possibility of a baby not surviving pregnancy or labor unless there are indications that there are problems. Sometimes even then, parents aren't informed. Pregnancy and childbirth are regarded as normal events. Many health care professionals go into the field for this very reason. When an elderly patient is admitted to the hospital with a heart attack or stroke, the staff may advise the family that there is a possibility their loved one may not survive. The family members are asked if there are advance directives, a set of written instructions for what a person desires to have done or not done in the event that the patient is unable to voice his or her wishes. These are very detailed and specific. When a healthy woman with a medically uneventful pregnancy enters the hospital full term in labor, nobody even considers, let alone suggests, that she may be going home alone. Nowhere is there a conversation or written information on the decisions parents must make, and the choices available, if their baby does not survive. Childbirth classes, if they discuss this topic at all, touch on it briefly. When I taught prepared childbirth classes in the early 1980's, toward the end of the series we spent some time discussing unwanted outcomes. It was brief and general and included things such as having a cesarean delivery. Today I am dismayed that anybody would consider a surgical delivery an unwanted outcome. It is certainly a disappointment if the couple had planned on a natural birth, but the thought that I included that situation in a discussion of premature babies, birth defects and neonatal death shames me. In talking to parents, I have heard it said many times "Nobody ever told me this could happen."

In her classic book *Education and Counseling for Childbirth Educators*, Sheila Kitzinger writes:

> Antenatal preparation at its most worthwhile educates and supports couples in coping with a life crisis. Sometimes that crisis is not what we expect it to be, and instead of the adjustment required when a healthy baby is born there are the other necessary adjustments to the reality of loss.

Unfortunately, not everybody appreciates what an impact the death of a baby has on parents and grandparents. This is a major traumatic event, and yet society tends to ignore it. Many people mistakenly believe that because nobody really "knew" the baby, it will be a relatively easy task to cope and move on. This attitude defies all of the years of research and literature about pregnancy and bonding. Many parents actually begin bonding with their baby before conception. If this was a planned pregnancy, as in the case of my son and daughter-in-law, the parents may talk before conception about what season they would like to deliver in, where they want to receive prenatal care, what their desires are for labor and delivery. They start sharing hopes and dreams. The bonding process between parent and child during pregnancy is intense. Mothers who miscarry early in the pregnancy grieve and mourn the loss of their baby. They don't think of it as a pregnancy loss-they have lost a child.

Parents get to know their child quite well during the pregnancy. My son and daughter-in-law both cried the first time they heard the baby's heartbeat. With the advent of ultrasound, parents are able to see their child while she is still in the womb. Tim and Jenn gave everyone framed pictures from the ultrasound scan, telling us "Here is your first baby picture." That picture is still sitting on my dresser. Some parents know the gender in advance and begin referring to the baby by name during the pregnancy. This baby is a very real part of their life, their plans for the future. Every decision made during the pregnancy takes into account the fact that there will be a child in the months to come-should I change jobs so I don't have to work as many nights, should we move to a larger place, if they are buying a home expectant parents will look into the school districts. The baby becomes paramount. As the baby grows and moves the parents really do experience their child. They know what kind of music their baby likes-Maddy used to dance to Dave Matthews. They talk to their baby and feel little knees and elbows. Their baby responds to the sound of their voices.

Many experts in the area of grief feel that the intensity of mourning is proportionate to the degree of intimate attachment, or bond, with the person who has died. In 1976, Marshall Klaus, M.D. and John Kennell, M.D., published their classic book titled *Maternal-Infant Bonding*. Klaus and Kennell were actually investigating the effects of separation of mother and newborn baby on the ability to bond. As they interviewed parents whose baby had died, they realized that the intense grief of these parents indicated a deep bonding that was initiated long before the birth.

Grandparents bond emotionally with their anticipated grandchild. Even though we don't feel every little kick and hiccup, we start thinking about the baby. We wonder if the baby will resemble our son or daughter. We also look forward to all of the things we are going to do with this new grandchild. We develop very specific hopes and dreams for how this baby will become a part of our lives. These anticipated events become the memories that we mourn when the baby dies. Obviously, one of the most difficult things to accept when a baby dies is that there are few memories to look back on, no special times to reminisce. This is a major difference between the death of a baby and that of an older person. One of the things people draw comfort from after the death of a parent or grandparent is sharing stories. It helps us to remember special times we spent together. Parents have the hard task of facing the lingering question of I wonder what my baby would be doing at one month, six months, etc. Would my baby be taking her first steps now? Grandparents think about these developmental milestones as well, but a large part of our grief journey involves facing the specific activities and events we had dreamed of sharing with the new grandchild. The first play I took my grandchildren to after Maddy's death was a bittersweet experience. I cherish every moment I spend with my grandchildren, and I was able to take pleasure in being at the play and seeing their excitement. However, I cannot deny that there was sadness with me that day; thoughts of how I dreamed of in a few years holding Maddy on my lap at a play.

One of the ways that family members remember their loved one is by talking about them. Parents who have experienced the death of a baby frequently say that one of their biggest fears is that nobody will remember their child. They want people to refer to the baby by name. They need to know that their baby is assured his or her place in the family. A grandparent can help to ensure that this occurs. I have repeatedly told my son and daughter-in-law how much I love Maddy. One of the things I said in my part of her eulogy was that my family doesn't count its members by their physical presence. I needed to state that publicly for my son and daughter-in-law to hear. I have three grandchildren. I say this not as a denial of her death, but to validate her life. When an older family member dies, we have lost part of our past. When a baby dies, we lose our future, our sense of immortality. Mourning lost hopes and dreams is an important task for grandparents.

Parents frequently say that the death of a baby changes them permanently. This is equally true of grandparents. For the parents, this may be their first intimate experience with death. Grandparents have more life experience and are more likely to have dealt with a death in the immediate family. Even so, the death of a baby makes us all stop and rethink our priorities. The grieving process is a transformation; we are not the same person we were. As a professional dealing with death in many forms and over many years, I knew on an intellectual basis that time would make this easier to bear. Yet emotionally, I couldn't imagine ever getting over Maddy's death. I realize that I will get through it, but I will never get over it. The psychosocial task of grieving is not to get over the loss, but to find a way to incorporate it into our life.

Burying a child or grandchild is the ultimate injustice life has to offer. It is death out of order. On some level we are aware that one day we will have to bury our grandparents or our parents. The fact that they will die, however unpleasant, is not totally unexpected. We are sad, we mourn the loss, and we miss them. Unless we lost a parent at a very young age, we have years of memories to help us cope with the grief. Many other people knew our loved one and can share stories with us. There are common memories of holidays, vacations, and special events. We are comforted by our memories. When a baby dies, it is another story entirely. The parents often feel as though they are the only ones who knew their baby. They may actually feel a closer bond to the medical staff that cared for them during the pregnancy and delivery because the nurses, doctors and midwives felt the baby, heard the baby's heartbeat, measured the baby's growth, and knew the intimate details of the pregnancy. I had conflicting emotions of jealousy and gratitude for the nurses and midwives who cared for Jenn. I was jealous because they knew Maddy so well, and yet it was a wistful jealousy, not a bitter one. Mostly, I was overwhelmingly grateful that my precious granddaughter knew that love and attention during her nine months in the womb, and that my son and daughter-in-law had that love and support during the pregnancy as well as the labor and delivery.

Along with learning more about the causes of stillbirth, the NICHD study is also investigating how to help families cope. The fact that a federal agency is looking into this problem gives recognition and validation to the fact that the death of a baby is a major trauma not only to the parents, but to the rest of the family as well. Grief counselors are part of the health professional team participating in the study. Perhaps this study will be able to answer some questions for those of us who need to know why this happened. A positive outcome would be the development of national standards for documenting and reporting stillbirth. It is past time for bereaved parents and grandparents to be encouraged to tell their story. The medical, therapeutic and social service community would do well to listen, because the families who have endured the death of a baby are the true grief experts. Grandparents need to be recognized as legitimate mourners and not only as a source of strength and support for our children. Our collective voice can serve as a force for change in a society that doesn't want to acknowledge our experience. By speaking out and sharing the intensely private thoughts and feelings of my grief journey, I hope that other grandparents will know that their tears will not be overlooked or forgotten.

CHAPTER 2

SHE WAS SIGNIFICANT

I wasn't supposed to be there. Tim and Jenn had put a great deal of thought into planning their birth experience. They did not want this event to be a three-ring circus. They were going to call the grandparents to join them after the baby was born. So many people, including my son, said to me "Oh yes you were" after hearing me tell them in an apologetic tone that I wasn't supposed to be there. Perhaps I wasn't supposed to be there, but I certainly was meant to be there.

"I need you to come and stay with Jenn. We had a baby girl. She doesn't have a heartbeat." Timothy stood before me in the waiting room of the Birth Center, and with those words, life as I knew it ceased to exist. I hurried up the stairs after my son, questions tumbling out, the nurse who had accompanied him down to me finally saying gently "We've called neonatal transport, we don't know what happened."

The story of Maddy actually began many months prior to this evening. My son Timothy and daughter-in-law, Jennifer had been married just short of two years. Tim called me himself one evening and said, "Hey mom how would you like to be a grandmother again?" I squealed back that he had better not be joking, that I would love it, that being a grandmother was the most wonderful thing in the world. Tim's older brother, Benjamin, has two children, and they are the absolute joys of my life. He assured me that he was not kidding; Jenn was indeed pregnant and due in November. I was overjoyed. As soon as I hung up from Tim, I started calling my closest friends to tell them my exciting news. I was already in love with this baby.

The next morning, I shared my news with several co-workers. There were six of us at the end of the floor where my office was located, and we are very close. We have shared many life passages.

The prior Easter, one of the women closest to me had lost her mother. Just a month earlier, another of this group had lost her husband after a long, hard fought, courageous battle with cancer. I chose to tell them of the pregnancy immediately because we all needed some good news, something happy to look forward to in the days ahead. They were thrilled.

As the months progressed I shared the pregnancy developments with my friends. They knew when Jenn first felt the baby move. Jenn met me for breakfast after an early morning checkup when the pregnancy was first becoming obvious, so my colleagues were able to meet her. I proudly displayed the framed ultrasound picture Tim and Jenn gave me.

The early ultrasound scan was unable to determine the gender, so Jenn took a urine DNA test. I was out of town attending a conference when Jenn got the results, and she called me on my cell phone. I announced to an elevator full of strangers that I was going to have a grandson. My co-workers, as well as family members, began to refer to the baby by name. I had no strong intuitive sense of whether the baby was a boy or a girl, but it seemed as though every time someone would ask me if we knew what it was, I would respond that they think it's a boy but I won't be convinced until the baby is born. I loved the girl's name they had chosen, but my secret preference wasn't gender based-I wanted this baby to have red hair. My mother, brother, sister and I all have red hair, as does my son, the expectant father.

Jenn had a glowing, medically uneventful pregnancy. She looked wonderful the entire time. A vegetarian, she was vigilant about nutrition. She read everything she could about pregnancy and childbirth. I bought something every week, a pack of diapers or box of wipes, throughout the pregnancy. As the summer drew to a close, I began to plan a baby shower with my other daughter-in-law. We included my six-year-old granddaughter in the plans to decrease any feelings of jealousy over the fact that she would no longer be the "baby" of the family. She helped us select the decorations and the color scheme. We decided that our shower would be small, immediate family, men included, a way to show Tim and Jenn that their baby was loved and eagerly awaited. My friends at work helped me make decisions about the wording on the cake. I wanted every aspect of the shower to be personal, to reflect my love for Tim and Jenn and their baby. I designed the invitations myself, using the pattern they had chosen for the nursery, hoping they would see the care and thought I had put into the plans. My bonding with this baby was already deep.

Jenn's due date was November 17th. I planned an early fall vacation taking this into consideration. While out west I purchased what I assumed would be the first of many t-shirts. I work with a small team consisting of two other women, the director of the program and our administrative assistant. We are quite close. They had actually written "Nina's grandbaby due" in our day timers, and every time we got together to go over calendars, it was included. As the day grew closer, I made sure the batteries in my digital camera were charged, and I began carrying the camera in my briefcase. I kept my personal cell phone charged and checked my messages frequently. My job requires that I am out of the office frequently, so starting the first week in November, I carried my cell phone and left it on vibrate, determined not to miss "the call." Prior to every workshop and meeting I excitedly explained why my cell phone was sitting in front of me.

Around five pm on Tuesday November 11 2003, Jenn called me. She said she was in labor. I immediately called a few of my closest friends and told them that the next time I spoke with them I would be a new grandmother! Jenn called back around six and told me that her water broke and that she had called Tim and he was on his way home from work. A few minutes later Tim called to tell me that Jenn was in labor. I was so pleased that he called me himself, just the way I was pleased when he called to tell me about the pregnancy. When I called my parents, my father told me that Tim had already called. He was tickled because Tim had also wished him a happy Veterans Day.

Tim and Jenn had decided that they did not want grandparents present for the labor and delivery. They would call us and we would join them after the baby was born, to share a toast and welcome our new grandchild. Figuring that this call would come in the middle of the night, I took a shower and washed my hair, wanting to be presentable the first time my grandchild saw me. I dozed off and on through the night. When morning came and I still hadn't received a call, I debated whether to go to work. The deciding factor for me was that the hospital where I work is only seven blocks from the Birth Center. When I got to work, I ran down the hall announcing that my daughter-in-law was in labor. I even told the housekeeping staff! I literally bounced up and down the hall in excitement and joy. I spoke with Tim and found out that they had been sent home the night before but were on their way back in. Tim promised to call me and keep me updated. I took those calls on my cell phone in the hallway so my co-workers could hear.

Later in the afternoon he called and said Jenn was six centimeters dilated. I said that when I got off work I was going to come over to the Birth Center. I told him I was old and tired and lazy, that I knew by the time I had battled with rush hour traffic to reach my home, about thirty minutes south, he would be calling me to turn around and come back into the city, again in rush hour traffic. This was out of character for me-I try to be very respectful of my adult children's decisions and plans. I don't want to be intrusive. Rarely do I insist on something contrary to their wishes. He didn't argue with me, which was out of character for him. I assured him that I did not expect to be with them during labor and delivery, that I had a book and would be content to sit in the waiting room.

I had been e-mailing my closest friends and family throughout the day, and the last e-mails I sent before I left the office said that the next e-mail or phone call they received would be coming from Grammy. I drove over to the Birth Center and settled in the waiting room after telling the receptionist who I was. Around four Tim came downstairs and told me he had seen my car and wanted to say hi. I gave him a hug and asked him to tell Jenn I love her.

The Birth Center finished seeing their regular appointments and closed up for the night. I was in the waiting room with my book, but I was too excited to concentrate on what I was reading. Shortly after five p.m. one of the nurses, Peggy, came down to tell me that Jenn was pushing and we would have a baby soon. I couldn't wait to hold my grandchild. When Tim came to me and begged me to stay with Jenn, my excitement instantly turned to dread. He said he was going to ride with neonatal transport and Maddy, and he wanted me to stay with Jenn and bring her to the pediatric hospital when she was discharged. I followed him up the stairs to the birthing suite, still unsure as to what was actually happening. My first thought was that Maddy's heart had stopped and she had been resuscitated. Then I thought maybe Tim mistakenly said heartbeat when he meant to say she wasn't breathing.

The scene I walked into was a nightmare I had never once contemplated. The entire staff was frantically working on my granddaughter, performing CPR and attempting to start her heart. I knew the minute I saw Maddy that she wasn't going to be revived. I went into autopilot mode. I turned from grandmother to healthcare professional, for to acknowledge the horror of what was taking place was more than I was capable of. I held Jenn's hand and stroked her hair from her face. I moved my son up by his wife's head and gave him her hand. Every fiber of my being was trying to will life into my granddaughter. My eyes danced back and forth from the clock to Maddy. I was aware that each minute that passed decreased the likelihood of her being revived. I was also aware that if the team was able to restore her heartbeat, there was almost no chance that she would be a healthy, normal baby. As Jenn's cries changed to moans of discomfort, I realized she was getting ready to deliver the placenta, and I assisted her. The neonatal transport team arrived and took over the CPR and resuscitation effort. The birthing suite, intended to be a welcoming setting of serenity and joy, had deteriorated into controlled chaos and barely concealed panic. The soft music chosen to accompany my grandchild's entrance into the world was replaced with the terse orders of the doctor. Finally, after the longest forty minutes of my life, the doctor called off the CPR and pronounced Maddy dead.

While the staff was completing paperwork and attending to Jenn, Tim asked me to make some phone calls. He begged me to call Jenn's mother. Jenn's family lives out of state. I called Jenn's mother, who was at work, and told her I would stay with Tim and Jenn. I called my mother and could barely get the words out. I called Michele, who has been my best girlfriend since my pregnancy with Tim. I quickly reached the point where I could not say the words one more time.

The caring and love exhibited by the staff was remarkable. They cried with us. Unable to release myself from the protective cone of healthcare worker, I found myself attempting to assess and comfort them. They put Maddy's footprints in the baby book, and cut a snip of her hair. Maddy was dressed in a pink dress and a cap was placed on her head. After asking Tim and Jenn if it was alright, I took pictures. I was crying and my hands were shaking so hard I could barely hold the camera steady. She was swaddled in a receiving blanket and given to her parents. Tim and Jenn held her and cried, and asked if I wanted to hold her. I carried her around, talking to her, crying, and kissing her. Jenn turned to me when she was asked which funeral home she wanted. I gave the name of a funeral director I have worked with, knowing that he would treat my son, daughter-in-law and granddaughter with dignity and respect. When the call was placed, the funeral director asked how much time the family needed. In an amazing display of grace and strength, Jenn replied "I need a lifetime." We wanted every minute we could possibly have with Maddy. Tim sat in the rocking chair cuddling his daughter. When Jenn was able, she also held and rocked her baby. We were able to hold her for several hours, trying to memorize her features and the feel of her in our arms. When the funeral director arrived, the staff removed the dress they had put on Maddy, laundered it and placed it in a memory box for Tim and Jenn. Jenn insisted on handing her baby directly to the funeral director. Tim told him "Take good care of my baby girl." And after nine months of life in the womb, twenty-six hours of labor, and several hours of holding Maddy, she was gone.

I begged Tim and Jenn to come home with me, but they wanted to go to Tim's brother's house. We left together and drove parallel down the turnpike until we reached the exit. I had called Michele as soon as I got in my car, and she talked to me during my drive home. It was the longest drive of my life. I have never felt so alone. I felt like a robot, automatically making the correct turns and somehow ending up in my driveway. I stretched out on my bed, wide awake, dreading the coming dawn, not knowing how to face a life without my granddaughter.

The next morning I nervously took the memory card from my digital camera and downloaded the pictures of Maddy. Because I was crying and trembling as I took them, I expected the pictures to be blurry and out of focus. When I opened the file to view them, I was astonished. Every single picture was in perfect focus. Little did I realize this was the beginning of a long stream of meaningful coincidences. I sobbed as I gazed at her perfect, beautiful features. This could not have happened. There was no way that this pregnancy, so wanted, so healthy, so well attended, could have ended in death. Her face in those pictures is serene. It is obvious there was no distress. Several people commented to me later that in one of the photos there appeared to be a glow around Maddy.

Jenn and I talked that day. Or perhaps it was the day after that. The time between Maddy's delivery and her funeral was blurred, one day running into the next without any conscious transition between night and day. Jenn said that when she first realized Maddy wasn't breathing, she thought they were going to have a sick baby, perhaps needing to be in intensive care, but that she and Tim could handle that. As CPR was being performed, Jenn told me she thought "OK, we are going to have a special needs child, but we have so much love to give her, so we will deal with that." A stillborn baby, never to hear her daughter cry, no child at all to parent, that was the one thing she never thought of, the thing she knew she and Tim could not bear.

The next few days passed in a fog. Flowers and meals arrived. I begged my parents and my oldest son and his family to come over and help eat the food. I remember thinking that it was ironic that a standard thing to do when there has been a death is to send food, yet I had absolutely no appetite. The phone rang nonstop. I have no idea who I talked to or what we talked about. I was numb. I moved through the days in slow motion. I am not a good sleeper to begin with, and now every time I started to drift off I had terrifying flashbacks of CPR being performed on Maddy. I heard the plaintive tone in my son's voice as he begged the staff to assure him his baby was going to be okay. Tim's anguished wail when he opened the car door and saw the infant car seat reverberated through me. I tried to use distraction therapy with myself and replace those scenes with her beautiful peaceful face as I held her. I wasn't able to cry when other people were around, and I really preferred being alone. I couldn't bear to hear any sound, even the voices of friends and family. I felt removed from their conversations, voices heard across a vast chasm, sounding as if they were underwater. None of my acquaintances had experienced this kind of loss, and I had nobody to talk to who understood the despair I felt.

I accompanied Tim and Jenn to the funeral home. Jenn's parents joined us, and we sat in the lobby while Tim and Jenn talked with the funeral director. The funeral director was stunned when he realized that I was there as a family member rather than in the role in which I had originally met him, that of a case manager accessing services for clients. The thought going through my head while I waited was that I should be meeting with a financial planner to open a college fund. Jenn's mother and I held hands as we sat. We were able to see Maddy. The funeral director reviewed our children's choices with us, and out of their hearing, I asked him to please send all correspondence to my house. I couldn't imagine my son having to open the bill for his daughter's funeral. Jenn's parents quickly told me they wanted to help. We had all driven separately, so I led Jenn's parents back to the turnpike, and then drove home alone yet once again.

The memorial service was a week away, on a Saturday. Tim and Jenn had decided to have Maddy cremated, and over the weekend they asked me if I would take some items to the funeral home to be cremated with her. They wanted to know if I could possibly go to the Birth Center Monday morning and get a piece of the monitor tracing, as Tim wanted to give Maddy her heartbeat back. They called the funeral home and asked for more of their daughter's hair. I suggested that perhaps they might like to put snips of their own hair in the urn, and they thought that was a good idea. I said I would pick up the tracing from the Birth Center and take it to the funeral home, and then bring them the hair. When I saw the staff at the Birth Center we all hugged and cried, unable to believe that Maddy was truly gone. In a poignant moment, we realized that this was Jenn's due date. In twenty-six years of operation, Maddy was the only stillbirth they experienced. My family believed our newest member would be unique, but this was not what we had in mind. I told the nurses and midwives how much I appreciated their love and the care they provided. After I left the funeral home, I stopped to sit with Pat. She had called me early that morning, and the minute I heard her voice I knew why she was calling. Her elderly aunt, who had lived with Pat's sister for years, had died that morning. Pat and I talked and laughed and cried together, and remarked on the irony of Aunt Helen and Maddy dying just days apart-one dying peacefully after a long, fully lived life, the other before she even drew a breath, truly the two extremes of life. Even though I was sad for Pat and her sister, this was a role I was familiar with. I knew how to provide comfort to others. What I didn't know was how to care for myself. I did not know how to even begin to mourn my granddaughter. Comforting Pat gave me a brief opportunity to deny my own grief.

The rest of that week was spent working on my eulogy. I had started a special journal for Maddy, and I used one of my first entries for the opening. I wrote and rewrote, trying to accurately express my feelings. Caught in a situation in which I could not fix things, this was one of the concrete things I could do. I dreaded the end of each day. I barely slept, feeling as though each new day carried me further away from my granddaughter. The funeral director called and spoke to me at great length about Tim and Jenn and Maddy. He also talked to Tim and Jenn, trying to get a sense of who they are so he could personalize the memorial service.

I was alternately overwhelmed with emotion and numb. I briefly talked to my oldest son and daughter-in-law about family counseling services offered through the funeral home for their children. I was unable to engage in any meaningful dialog with them about having their children attend the funeral. I felt disconnected from the rest of my family. Every iota of energy I possessed was spent getting through the motions of the day, leaving nothing to offer to my remaining grandchildren.

Maddy's service was personal and meaningful. After consulting with Tim and Jenn, I had enlarged, printed and framed one of Maddy's pictures, which sat on an easel at the front of the room. We wanted her picture displayed as a way of showing everybody that Maddy was a person, not a pregnancy loss. Her urn was on a table, surrounded by candles we used in a family ritual of inclusion and unity. The funeral director used the phrase "she was significant" as his theme, repeating it over and over. He managed to capture and share the essence of what Maddy meant to our family. Tim and Jenn had prepared remarks, which Tim read. I gave my eulogy, followed by the candle lighting ceremony. Tim and Jenn wanted to be alone after the service, so I busied myself with my brother, who had flown in the night before from Colorado, and my best girlfriend, who drove down from out of state the morning of Maddy's service.

My brother left for his flight home shortly after brunch the following day, and a few hours later my girlfriend also left. As I sat alone in the late afternoon hours, the sky gradually darkening as day moved toward night, I realized there was nothing left for me to do but grieve. I spent the next few days searching the internet for information, both on stillbirth and grief. I found many books and articles on stillbirth and parental bereavement, but almost nothing for grandparents. Hours were devoted to chronicling my emotions in my journal. I surrounded myself with parental bereavement books, devouring them nonstop. I ordered two books on grandparent grief. One of them turned out to be a pamphlet, and I cried in despair, wanting more. Several of the parental bereavement books briefly addressed grandparents and I sobbed in frustration that my grief was so meaningless as to not deserve greater mention. It certainly did not feel meaningless. I didn't sleep. I barely ate. I turned to my journal more and more, rereading passages. I made the sarcastic comment to my daughter-in-law that my journal entries were the book I wanted to read, and at that moment *Forgotten Tears* came into being. Six weeks after Maddy was born still, I began formalizing a book on the grief journey as experienced by a grandparent. My son and daughter-in-law encouraged and supported my writing from the bottomless pit of their own grief. The significance of a baby girl who never drew a breath is astonishing.

Maddy shares a birthday with a legendary woman. Elizabeth Cady Stanton, born on November 12 1815, co-founded the women's rights movement. She was the first president of the National Woman's Suffrage Association. With her staunch feminist mother and her social activist grandmother, I have no doubt that, given the opportunity, Maddy would have fulfilled the destiny conferred on her by this shared birth date.

Timothy and Jennifer's Remarks at Maddy's

Memorial Service

On Wednesday, November 12, 2003, at 6:17 p.m., our beautiful daughter, Maddy, came into the world, and seven hours later we came home without her. It has been two weeks since then, although it gets hard to tell one day from the next. I never understood what people meant when they said, "I remember it like it was yesterday" until now. It will always seem like yesterday that, after twenty-six hours of labor, we finally got to see her beautiful face. She had my big ears and my wife's big feet. She had a head full of brown hair, but dark red eyelashes, and the cutest little nose. We are amazed that we could create something beautiful and perfect.

When we went into labor, we knew that our lives were going to be changed forever that day, but we had no idea it would be like this. We had done our best to make a good home for her. We had everything she needed-love, warmth, and the safety of two parents who wanted her more than anything. We even plugged in the wipes warmer on the way to give birth so that when she came home, her little bottom wouldn't catch a chill when we changed her diaper. I would give anything for the chance to change one dirty diaper. Jennifer and I spoke constantly of the day we would get to bring her home, but never did we think we would be bringing our daughter home like this.

We feel very lucky for the time we got with her, but robbed of the time we did not. We got to know that Maddy hates Chinese food and red peppers, and loves to dance to Dave Matthews. Jennifer always said that Maddy would wake up and start kicking when I came home and she heard my voice. We used to play with her, poking Jennifer's belly and she would kick us back. We cherish the time and the memories that we have, and the knowledge that in her short life, she had more than most people do-a warm safe home, where love is unconditional.

In the past ten days, Maddy has taught us a lot about life and taught us how much we love each other. She has shown us small things in life are to be treasured. She is already making us better people through her very existence, and that is her legacy.

Sometimes I feel guilty to smile when I think of her, but I will not believe that Maddy wants her dad to cry. I would give anything for just one scribbled drawing of hers, or to get a "Number One Dad" Father's Day card she made me at school. We would give anything to be able to push her on a swing, or play peek-a-boo. I have a daughter and her name is Madeline. I am a good dad and my wife is a good mom. We're going to bring our baby home today.

Nina's Remarks at Maddy's Memorial Service

Joy is contagious, it lifts you up like a balloon, and others are eager to share. Grief, on the other hand, is a heavy weight that pulls you under, and nobody is comfortable being confronted with a friend's grief. The Bennett, Skahan and Hodgdon families are blessed that so many of our friends and colleagues have chosen to share this with us. It is your support that will give us the strength to endure what seems unbearable. Thank you for being with us today.

My own grief is compounded by the desire to alleviate my son's pain. When he was little and fell down I could pick him up. When he fell off his bike and scraped his knee I could put a band-aid on and kiss him and make it better. But I can't make this better. I am confronted with something I can't fix. I would willingly bear my son's pain, but I can't even do that for him.

What I am able to do is honor my beautiful granddaughter Madeline by telling you a little bit about her parents. My son Timothy and daughter-in-law Jennifer are an incredible couple. They have demonstrated an amazing degree of strength and courage throughout, and at a time when the older generations traditionally should have been role models, it is Tim and Jenn who have led the way and taught us so many lessons. When I stated how proud I have been of how my son has handled his loss and how guilty I felt because it took a tragedy for me to see what a fine man he has become, his father very kindly assured me that I always knew in my heart, I merely lost sight of it during the teenage years. How often do we really see our children as distinct and separate adults? I can honestly say that one of the lessons for me in this has been a new and impressive view of my son. He is every bit the man of my hopes and dreams.

C.S. Lewis said that grief is a journey along a winding road. As you round each bend you have no idea what lies ahead. Tim and Jenn share a love that will enable them to face tomorrow. That love has become the fortress that will permit them to eventually heal.

When you think of my son and daughter-in-law, I don't want you to remember the grief and tears. Please don't think of them with sadness. I'd like to ask you instead to think of the dignity and grace with which Tim and Jenn have embarked on this journey. I am confident that around one of those bends there will again be laughter and joy. Each of us will rediscover purpose and meaning in our lives. Tim and Jenn are part of a family that doesn't count its members by their physical presence. Maddy will always be a part of me. She will never be forgotten. Every breeze that touches my cheek will be my granddaughter whispering secrets. Every fluffy cloud that floats across the sky is a kiss I am sending her. I will see her in every soft sunrise and brilliant sunset. And when I'm in Colorado and feel a snowflake on my face, I know that Maddy will be telling me it's time to stop crying. Maddy, I loved you from the moment I knew you existed. I will always love you.

So when you think of me, please don't think of my heart being heavy with grief. Instead, think of my heart overflowing with love for my family. Think of my heart full of gratitude and appreciation for the support of my friends. Live every day to it's fullest. And when you see stars twinkling on a clear night, remember our Maddy, and smile.

CHAPTER 3

THE GRIEF JOURNEY

Grief teaches the steadiest minds to waver

Antigone
Sophocles

In late September 2003, I went to Colorado to spend a week with my brother and sister-in-law. I had timed the vacation carefully, as Tim and Jenn were due mid-November. I spent a wonderful week, full of joy and anticipation for my new grandchild. I even bought her a t-shirt when I was shopping for my other grandchildren. The last night I was there Judy Collins was doing a discussion and book signing to promote her new book, *Sanity and Grace*. She had been a favorite artist of mine in the sixties, and I was thrilled to be able to see her in person. The afternoon of the signing I bought her book without having any idea what it was about; it is an intensely emotional account of her life and the events leading to her son's suicide, as well as her journey through grief afterward. I read the entire book that afternoon, unable to tear myself away. During the discussion that evening she talked about what a social taboo suicide is and how the inability of society to openly address the topic isolates surviving family members. I thought she was incredibly brave and strong to be able to share her deepest thoughts. My brother teased me about being a groupie as he watched me eagerly standing in line for Judy Collins to sign my book. When it was my turn, I thanked her for being able to talk about a subject as difficult as suicide. Not once did I think that in six weeks I would be undergoing a tragic nightmare of my own. I never imagined that not even two months after hearing her talk about the death of her son, I would be joining her on a journey I never wanted to take, one which also is not discussed, thus leaving grieving

24

family members without the social support they so desperately need. Within days of Maddy's death I adopted Both Sides Now as my theme song.

The death of a loved one is the most stressful event anyone will encounter. The death of a baby is the ultimate tragedy. The word bereavement means to be deprived by death, and that is exactly how parents feel. They have been deprived. They have been cheated. The National Mental Health Association states in a fact sheet that a child's death arouses an overwhelming sense of injustice. Parents dreamed and planned and prepared for a baby. They endured the physical and emotional changes of pregnancy with the belief that it would all be worthwhile. Expectant parents are taught in prenatal classes that the pain of labor contractions fades because there is a reward at the end-a baby. Not only have parents had their hopes and dreams shattered, they have quite literally lost a part of themselves. On the third anniversary of the 9/11 terrorist attacks, Mayor Michael Bloomberg of New York talked about the fact that there is no common name for a parent or grandparent who has suffered the death of a child. Our society validates other losses by publicly acknowledging a person's new status. A person whose spouse has died is either a widow or a widower. A child whose parents have died is an orphan. We even validate the loss of a marriage with the term divorcee. The horror of having a child die is so great, so unimaginable, that we don't have a name for the condition.

Grief is a normal response to loss. The more significant the loss, the more intense the grief will likely be. The process of grieving requires time, patience, courage and support. There is a wide range of emotional and physical reactions. It is imperative to grieve in order to integrate the death into your being and continue living. Beliefs and attitudes about death, especially the death of a baby, will influence grieving. Medical staff used to believe, because this is what they were taught, that parents should not see a dying or dead baby. The baby was taken out of the delivery room immediately. In many cases, parents who asked to see their child were told, "You really don't want to do that." Parents were given little information, sometimes not even knowing whether their baby was a girl or a boy. Mothers were heavily sedated during labor if serious problems were suspected, and they were kept sedated for several days afterward, making it difficult if not impossible to arrange or even attend a funeral service. I was working as a childbirth educator during the years when many of these attitudes were being challenged. Professionally, I have seen firsthand the difference it makes when the enormity of the parents' loss is acknowledged openly. Today, most medical staff are aware of the importance of seeing and holding the baby, taking pictures and creating memories. Dr. Michael Berman, in a press release issued by the M.I.S.S. Foundation in response to a study published in the British medical journal Lancet, states "I advocate and encourage my patients to see, hold, bond with and caress their newly born children-for as long as they need- who are not born alive. In over 30 years of personal experience with this approach, I have never been sorry and have only received positive responses from my patients...I have also spoken with and cared for patients who have experienced these losses and were not offered the opportunity to see or hold their children and they regrettably wished they had." Unfortunately, sometimes it is friends or family members, who will, through their attitude toward the death of a baby and insensitive comments, make the grieving process even more difficult.

There is no template for grief. It is a very individual experience. People will express their grief differently. C.S. Lewis said that grief is a journey along a winding road. As you round each bend, you have no idea what lies ahead. Personally, I like this concept. I refer often to my grief journey. This is a trip I never wanted to take. There is no road map to guide me along this journey. However, I realize that it is only by making my way around the twists and turns that I will find peace. There is also no time line for grief. There is no magic formula that says in so many months you are healed. Too often, we find that others have expectations of how long it is appropriate to grieve, and when we don't meet those expectations it only serves to compound our feelings of inadequacy.

Sandy Hoffman, whose grandson was stillborn, states in an article in the AGAST newsletter "This is truly a journey of endurance, compassion, frustration, faith, anger, and love. We feel alone and the solitude is formidable. People who aren't on this journey don't understand, and mean well when they tell us 'to get on with life'."

I devoured these words the first time I read them, taking them into my heart. This was exactly how I felt-completely and totally alone. Although I have several people close to me who offered me love and empathy, I still felt as though nobody really understood what I was feeling. I felt so isolated. I had changed, I was a different person, and nobody seemed able to see that. People talked to me in the same way as before. The world continued on as though nothing had happened. There were days when I wanted to scream "Can't you see that I'm not the same?" A broken limb is encased in a cast and everyone seeing it realizes that there has been some kind of injury. People expect there to be a lengthy healing process, perhaps involving physical therapy to recover full use of the limb. It's an openly acknowledged topic of conversation-total strangers will offer sympathy when they see a cast. A broken heart is invisible on the outside, which makes it easy for others to deny or forget the pain a bereaved person feels. The pain was all consuming. Liz, the mother of a stillborn son, told me "It only hurts when I breathe."

Because the emotions we feel after a baby dies are so intense and painful, we may try to avoid them. Grandparents may notice their son or daughter withdrawing, not wanting to see them or talk. Friends and other family members may try to get the grieving parents to go out, to socialize, when they would prefer to be left alone. This desire for solitude can be mistaken for isolation. This is incredibly difficult for the grandparent, who needs to spend time with their son or daughter for their own healing. We need assurance that our child is not sinking into clinical depression. The first few days after Maddy died my desire to spend time with my son and daughter-in-law was overwhelming. It seemed as though every time I called them they would put me off. My need to be with them was soon overcome by my need for reassurance that they were not suicidal. Fortunately for me, my older son's wife stayed in close touch with me. I soon realized that my son and daughter-in-law were not isolating themselves, but were asking to be with people when they needed companionship. I was able to talk to my son and tell him I would respect his need for quiet time with his wife if he would assure me that when they needed to talk they would pick up the phone. The first time my daughter-in-law called me we talked and cried for nearly an hour. Some of my tears were ones of gratitude that she had reached out to me-I felt as though I was finally being helpful.

As early as 1917, Sigmund Freud discussed grief. His basic premise was that emotional attachments are what hold individuals together, so grief is the process of detaching from the relationship with the person who has died. John Bowlby expanded on Freud's ideas and stated that grief is an adaptive response to loss. He also stated that it is an active process that takes time. Colin Murray Parkes described grief in terms of psychosocial transition. He talks about repeatedly going over the loss in one's mind, and attempting to make some sense of the death. Elizabeth Kubler Ross, in her landmark book *On Death and Dying*, first published in 1969, described five stages dying patients go through. She believed that grief is a normal, natural process. William Worden takes the stages theory even further, and identifies four tasks that bereaved persons need to accomplish. His third task, adjusting to an environment that has changed because of the loss, is particularly difficult for parents whose baby died. The adjustment they need to make involves their self-identity, which for many months may have been defined by the anticipation of parenthood. He states that even though people regain an interest in life and reinvest their emotional energy in new activities and relationships, mourning is a long-term process, which may never really be finished. More recently, Nancy Moos points out that grief does not occur in isolation, and that it is necessary to work through grief from the viewpoint of family dynamics. She states that the interaction and communication patterns between family members may be disrupted by death. Roles within the family shift or change, sometimes permanently.

In the aftermath of events such as the school shootings at Columbine and the terrorist activities of 9/11, attention has been paid to the impact of trauma and how it intensifies the reactions to sudden, unexpected death. Therese Rando is a psychotherapist who has written extensively on issues of death and bereavement. While she has not focused exclusively on the death of a baby, much of her writing is applicable. She believes that sudden, unanticipated death casts an overlying layer of trauma on the loss. The bereaved person's emotional responses are intensified; he or she may even exhibit symptoms of posttraumatic shock. In a paper published in 1996 she remarks that "the suddenness and lack of anticipation of the death overwhelm the mourner," leaving little resources for coping. This made a great deal of sense to me. What could possibly be more unexpected and traumatic than presenting in labor after a perfectly normal full term pregnancy, and twenty-four hours later coming home facing funeral preparations?

I came across writings exploring the concept of disenfranchised grief in the 1990s when I was teaching bereavement workshops for community based agencies working with clients with HIV/AIDS. Dr. Kenneth Doka first used the term in 1989. A disenfranchised loss is, quite simply, a loss that society does not recognize. This may occur because society doesn't recognize the relationship between the mourner and the deceased, as in the case of a gay man whose lover has died. Or it may be that society doesn't recognize the loss as being significant, which is often what happens in the case of miscarriage or stillbirth. Nancy, whose grandson Ethan was born prematurely and lived for 24 hours, says "I was taken by surprise at just how much it hurts to lose a grandchild. There is a point where your chest actually hurts and you can hardly breathe. And yet, the world doesn't even acknowledge that grandparents have the right to grieve. We grieve alone." Everybody is made uncomfortable by the death of a baby; it leaves us all shaken and keenly aware of our vulnerability. Many people are uncertain of what to do or say, so in effect they discount the loss by ignoring it. Grandparents are faced with a double whammy when considering the concept of disenfranchised grief and its effects. We are seen not as mourners, but in our parental role as strong, supportive caregivers for our bereaved children. We then receive little social support as a result of the lack of validation for the intense emotions we are feeling. Literature on both trauma and grief reports that social support is crucial.

Bits and pieces of these different theories appealed to me as I studied them. None of them, however, seemed to accurately capture what I was experiencing. One of the inherent dangers with any model is that it will be taken as a prescription for grieving, and when the person hasn't reached the next stage he or she feels as though they are doing something wrong. One of the issues I explored was the disconnect between what I knew intellectually and what I was feeling. My bereavement training had been in the traditional stages models, in particular the concept promoted by Kubler Ross. I had been comfortable with the idea of stages because they gave a sense of order to the chaos of bereavement. As a healthcare professional, stages were something concrete I could describe to people dealing with the death of a loved one. Yet when I was faced with the death of my granddaughter, I didn't feel as though the stages had much relevance to what I was experiencing. It helped somewhat to read about the many intense emotions I was experiencing; seeing the written descriptions validated my right to those emotions. I found the entire concept of resolution disturbing. How could I possibly resolve the loss of my granddaughter? And even more important, did I really want to resolve this? Resolution implies acceptance and moving on. The fact that Maddy had not survived delivery is unacceptable. According to the stages theory of grief, if I don't resolve and accept my granddaughter's death I run the risk of pathological grief. Margo, whose grandson Peyton was stillborn, says that the concept of acceptance has been the most difficult part of the grief journey for her. She refused to accept that her precious grandson is gone, although she certainly does realize the undeniable fact of his death.

Stages can provide a starting point for understanding the complexity of the grieving process. Dr. Doka states that the stage models lead to myths about grief, such as the belief that recovery and resolution are expected and even desirable.

Journal entry:
> I don't know which I'm more afraid of-that I'll never get over her or that I will. It still hurts so badly. I feel so isolated because the people closest to me don't

seem to have any idea of how much I am hurting. I have never felt so alone in my life.

Theorists are questioning the traditional stage models of grief. Dr. Robert Neimeyer is a psychologist who has written prolifically on bereavement issues. His research on grief has led him to believe that most models and theories of grief are inadequate because they fail to recognize the individuality of bereavement. The concept of predictable stages and phases assumes that there is a readily identifiable endpoint. The final stage, frequently called recovery or resolution, implies that a bereaved person gets over the loss. Neimeyer uses what is called constructivist psychotherapy, which sees grieving as a process of rebuilding meaning in a life that has been challenged by the loss. He states that the goal of grieving is not to let go, but to find a way to hold on with less pain. Grieving is seen as a way to redefine normal in a world that is drastically and permanently different. In an article on the five myths of grief written for the Grief Digest, Dr. Alan Wolfelt says the fifth myth is the belief that the goal is to get over your grief. He states that we don't resolve or recover from grief, but rather, we learn how to reconcile our grief. Many contemporary therapists and grief theorists say that grief is a lifelong process. It never completely ends, although the intense emotions ease over time; our grief becomes a part of who we are.

Dr. Kathleen Gilbert is an Associate Professor with the Department of Applied Health Science at Indiana University. She teaches a web class called Grief in a Family Context. In the first unit, What is Grief? Dr. Gilbert says "Grief is much more than a person's emotional response to a loss. It is the totality of the response. Grief includes emotions and thoughts and is contradictory and confusing: Bereaved feel a need to be a part of something and to be apart from everything; the need to feel deeply and to avoid feelings; the need to talk and to be silent. Grief is the state of being that results from the recognition that the world that "should be" is different from the world that is- a world that is forever changed by the loss." Friends and family members may have difficulty comprehending that our personal world as well as our view of the world at large has changed. There is no visible outward sign to remind people of our loss.

Even though people grieve differently, and express their grief in different ways, there is some commonality to the emotional reactions that bereaved people experience. Psychologists and others who have studied bereavement and grief generally agree that the process of grieving consists of shock, suffering and renewal. These phases are not orderly, and people often go back and forth between them. Every bereaved person does not necessarily experience every emotional reaction. It is also possible to have a mix of phases. There are many behavioral and emotional responses associated with each phase. Again, there is no set amount of time for working through the various reactions. There is also no right or wrong way to grieve. Every bereaved person must find his or her own way through the pain, and people supporting grieving parents and grandparents need to respect the individuality of grieving.

Usually the first response to being told that the baby has died is shock. This is often described as feeling physically and emotionally numb. Emotional numbing is the mind's instinctive way of protecting us from overload. It is difficult to make decisions. Every time a friend would ask me if I was hungry, I said I wasn't. When somebody set food in front of me, I ate automatically. I would call my mother and beg her to come over to my house, and shortly after she arrived I wanted her to leave. Quite simply, I didn't know what I wanted. Actually, I did know-I wanted Maddy back, and I knew that nothing anybody could do would accomplish that. Feelings of disbelief are common. The death doesn't seem real. The first few mornings after Maddy died, my first thought when I awoke was that it was a new day and we were going to do it all again, and this time it would turn out differently. I found myself not wanting to go to bed at night, not wanting it to be another day, feeling as though each day took me further away from Maddy. Some people may feel the opposite- they can't wait for each day to be over, to distance them from the nightmare of the death.

Everyday life seems chaotic and disorganized. Grieving people often feel as if they are losing their mind. I would wander from room to room, I was forgetful, and I was unable to complete simple tasks. I couldn't concentrate-I am a voracious reader, but I would find myself staring at the same page of the book an hour after I sat down. I couldn't tolerate noise of any kind- I couldn't bear to have the television on, and after a few minutes even the conversation of friends and family became too much. I found it difficult to follow a conversation. I would alternate from bursts of frantic energy to periods of lethargy, when the mere act of standing up and walking across the room seemed to be more than I could manage. Many months later I still found it unpleasant to be in noisy social situations. I much preferred spending quiet time with a few friends.

Harriet Sarnoff Schiff, in her wonderful book *The Bereaved Parent*, says:

> The numbness stayed with me for days and would come in waves just as my weeping and sorrow would come in waves. For that, a grieving parent can be thankful. If we had to face the enormity of our loss for every waking minute, I am certain it would completely envelop us and consume us and prevent us from ever again becoming whole.

I have the 1977 edition of this book, purchased during my years as a childbirth educator. It made such an impression that I remembered the author's name after all these years, and bought a new edition for my daughter-in-law and son to have. The author's honest words have provided comfort for bereaved parents for nearly thirty years, and helped them realize that they are not alone.

As the numbness wore off I found myself longing for Maddy. I cried out that I wanted to hold her again, I wanted to kiss her one more time, and I wanted to tell her how much I love her. I could still feel the weight of her in my arms. The pain I felt was excruciating. I actually physically ached to hold that baby. I paced my house with my arms in a cradling position, similar to the way I paced the Birth Center with Maddy the night she was born. Except now my arms were empty. Disbelief set in. It didn't seem possible that after all these months of planning and excitement there was no baby to hold.

Waves of sadness swept over me. My life seemed empty and devoid of meaning. I wanted to help my son and he seemed to be holding himself back from me. I knew intellectually that he was heartbroken, that he was not rejecting me, but I overreacted to everything. This is generally called the suffering phase. I have also heard this time referred to as the phase of emotional release. The numbness wears off and we become aware of just how dreadful the loss is. Every day seems like an emotional roller coaster. The pain must be faced and felt. This is usually the longest stretch of the grief journey. Friends and family mean well when they tell us that time heals, but the words are meaningless because we know this is a wound that time can't touch. We may find that at some point during our suffering friends seem to feel as though it's gone on long enough. I felt as though I were in slow motion, as though I had stopped moving, yet life continued on around me. All I wanted to talk about was Maddy-my suffering was the extent of my reality. Tom Golden, LCSW, is a psychotherapist who specializes in healing from loss and trauma. He has published many articles as well as a book on bereavement issues. He states "Many times we have a sense that there is no way out of the situation, that the grief we are experiencing is never going to end. Part of a significant grief is the feeling that the grief has become the only reality and will continue forever." It is important that bereaved people and those providing comfort realize that these feelings and experiences are normal. Gerry Trickle, in an article I found on the internet, writes "A grieving person's entire being- emotional, physical and spiritual, is focused on the loss that just occurred. Grief is a 100% experience. No one does it at 50%." It takes all of our time and all of our energy to grieve. This can make it difficult to focus on routine activities. Other problems that occur may seem monumental when added to the weight of the grief journey. When you are emotionally depleted, it is overwhelming to face one more decision or family issue. Nerves are frayed, emotions volatile, and our usual coping skills may not be readily available.

The grief would attack me without warning. There seemed to be no identifiable trigger for when the tears would come. Some days I couldn't seem to stop crying, and other days the tears refused to fall.

We have long heard that tears are therapeutic, and recently some psychologists and scientists have been conducting research in an attempt to determine if there is indeed a difference between tears produced from an irritant and tears resulting from strong emotions. William Frey is a biochemist that has studied the chemical makeup of tears. His discovery that tears produced by emotional stimuli contained more total protein than tears caused by an irritant led him to postulate that emotionally based tears contain high levels of cortisol. Cortisol is a hormone released under stress, so perhaps crying is nature's way of eliminating toxins. People frequently report that crying has a cleansing effect. Ironically, crying is not something our society encourages. Crying is often equated with weakness or a loss of control, rather than recognition that our tears are an outward expression of the emotions coursing through us. We need to be careful not to use crying as a measurement of grief. Some people cry much more readily than others. Just because a person doesn't cry does not mean that they are not feeling the pain of the loss. The person who sobs frequently is not out of control. People around us may be uncomfortable witnessing our tears, but we need to be allowed to shed them. We also may not be at ease crying openly in front of others. For the most part, I did not cry when I talked about what had happened to my family. I cried in the shower. I cry when I am alone in my house. I sobbed almost every morning during my commute to work-I was emotionally drained by the time I arrived at my office. Most of my crying was, and still is, done in the car. Driving has always been mental health time for me, a chance to review the day, an opportunity to think about things without interruption.

Journal entry:
>Rough day. I cried all the way home from work. The only time I am able to cry is when I am alone. I feel as though I have to be tough and strong in front of others. I am drowning in a sea of silent tears.

What I didn't expect was that I would still be crying several months after Maddy died. I generally tend to cry more out of anger than sadness. I was disappointed in myself, feeling that I should be able to control my emotions better than I was doing. The UC counseling center web site has a wonderful article on grief, which states "society often encourages people to quickly move away from grief. Unfortunately, refusing to cry, suffering in silence, and "being strong" are often viewed as admirable and desirable reactions to loss. Many people have internalized the idea that grieving and mourning should be done quickly, quietly, and efficiently." People will make comments like "She's such a trouper" or "He's a rock" in tones of respect and admiration. How often do we hear somebody say "Isn't it good that she can get her grief out?" when we start to cry? People are uncomfortable witnessing any strong emotional expression, so they are quick to praise those who keep their emotions to themselves.

Many times anger is also a response during this phase. Anger toward the medical establishment is a normal and understandable reaction. With all of the medical technology and knowledge available, there is a general expectation that medical staff is omnipotent. Grandparents may find themselves in the awkward position of fielding inquiries about the quality of the medical care. Because I was present and also because of my expertise in the prenatal field, I received several phone calls questioning the care Jenn and Maddy had received. At a time when I needed consolation for my loss, I found myself defending the excellent care given to my daughter-in-law and granddaughter. It is difficult to direct and deal with anger when there is no identifiable cause for the baby's death. There is a very real potential for self-destructive behavior, such as substance abuse, when the anger can't be released. Grandparents can be instrumental in assisting our children to direct the anger constructively. Anger is as difficult an emotion to witness as grief, but we can help our children by encouraging them to talk about any feelings of anger. We may also feel angry- angry that our child is experiencing such pain, angry that our family is going through this. Our anger may be directed at a society that seems to feel that as grandparents we have little basis for prolonged mourning. For many grandparents, anger can be mixed with guilt. Grandparents who live far from their child may have been asked not to come for the birth, but to come a bit later and help with the new baby. Or we may have been offered the choice and decided to come after the baby was home. We may not be in a financial position to travel yet suddenly find ourselves spending money we can't spare for plane tickets to attend our grandchild's funeral. The guilt can be as fundamental as recognizing that our grandchildren are not supposed to die before us. Standing in the birthing room watching the medical staff, one of my first thoughts was that I would willingly give my life if my granddaughter could live. The mantra running through my head was "not her, not her, take me instead." Maddy's maternal great-grandmother tearfully said, "It should have been me."

Many people take refuge in their faith and religious beliefs during times of crisis. Others find themselves angry with God. I have always been somewhat envious of those who appear able to accept that God has a reason for everything. I consider myself to be a spiritual person, but not particularly religious. During one of my earliest attempts to socialize, an acquaintance commented that God had a purpose in taking Maddy. I'm sure she meant to comfort me, but her words angered me. I told her that no God I could ever possibly believe in would take a baby. I was angry that Jenn had to endure the physical changes that accompany childbirth. It seemed like the ultimate cruelty when her milk came in. If there was some kind of reason or master plan for this tragedy, shouldn't her body have been informed? Many people made comments to me based on their own religious beliefs, not realizing that these remarks only isolated me more because they did not reflect my beliefs.

Our society places unrealistic and unfair expectations and pressures on men. To again quote Harriet Sarnoff Schiff, "Nowhere in all the annals of sex discrimination is there a more glaring injustice than that thrust upon a bereaved father." The role of the father during pregnancy and childbirth has expanded to be as inclusive as possible. Men accompany their partners to prenatal checkups. They are present in the exam room when the heartbeat is heard. They are present during an ultrasound, and are able to actually see their child moving about in the womb. They attend prepared childbirth classes and expect to have an active role during the labor and delivery. Many companies offer paternity leave. For all the progress we've made with increasing the involvement of fathers during pregnancy, childbirth and child rearing, we still see fathers in the stereotypical role of provider and source of strength. The grieving father has endured the greatest tragedy imaginable, and he is then expected to get dressed and go to work as though nothing has happened. The way we define manhood is extremely limiting. Fathers often feel personal guilt over their perceived failure to not only protect their wife but also their child. When they do return to work, they are extremely conflicted because they feel guilty about leaving their wife to face the day alone. The pressure they experience may seem overwhelming. Grandfathers may have difficulty helping their sons with these feelings, because in general men are not encouraged to relate to one another on an emotional level. Despite the many advances in equality between males and females, it is still not common for men to cry. Not only are men uncomfortable with their tears, the women who love them are also uneasy. As the mother of sons, I was resentful with the expectations of friends and family members that my son needed to get right back to work. He needed to cry, he needed to grieve, and he needed to be encouraged and supported in his mourning. Because of the complexities of the mother-son relationship, I felt as though my hands were tied in supporting him. He needed to hear these things from another man, a man he respected and trusted.

There may be physical reactions to grief, including fatigue, changes in sleep patterns, and alterations in appetite. In the Compassionate Friends brochure, The Grief of Grandparents, there is a paragraph titled Grief Work. Grief is hard work, and hard work is exhausting. This is another aspect I wasn't prepared for. I felt mentally, emotionally and physically drained. I don't recall ever having been so tired in my life. Even when I got a full night's sleep, which wasn't often, I did not feel rested. Adequate, restful sleep is the foundation for good health, both physical and mental. I was forgetful. I found it difficult to focus and concentrate for any amount of time. I worried that people around me would become impatient with me. To a large extent, I bought into society's attitude that grief is something to be done with quickly. I felt guilty because I couldn't seem to bounce back and get over my loss. The more I read about grief, the more I realized that grief is something to be experienced, not something to overcome. It was only by allowing the pain to rise to the surface that I could begin to let it out.

Journal entry:
> I feel completely drained. I am consumed with grief; it has become my very being. I want a magic potion to make the pain go away. I don't want to talk about anything else but Maddy. I feel as though I am letting people down because I am not the same person I was before 6:17 pm November 12. It's so hard not knowing if it will be a good day or a bad day. It's almost as though my mind shuts down to protect me, which is good, but I never know when that's going to happen, which isn't so good. I'm doing the best that I can. Some days that's a lot better than others.

There is a strong sense of disbelief. This differs from the numbing shock felt when the death first occurs. It isn't a denial; it's almost a questioning. How could this have happened? Why did this happen to our family? How can I possibly go on, how can anything have meaning after this? I knew that Maddy had not survived delivery, yet somehow I just couldn't believe it. It was incomprehensible. I actually walked through my house thinking that this couldn't be real. It was not possible that this had happened to my family. Four months after my granddaughter was born still, I received a phone call telling me that a former co-worker's son and daughter-in-law had just delivered a stillborn boy. When I called Mary, she kept asking "Why?" Harold Kushner, in his book *When Bad Things Happen to Good People*, states that why is not a question, but a cry of pain. Even though in many cases the question remains unanswered, we still feel a need to ask it over and over. My daughter-in-law summed it up perfectly when she said that even if we knew *what* happened to cause Maddy's death, we still wouldn't know *why*.

Maddy's stillbirth left me feeling particularly vulnerable to the unpredictability of life. It challenged my beliefs about right and wrong, and it drastically reminded me how little control we really have over anything. There is a general expectation that we have a large degree of control over life events. If we get good grades in high school, we will be accepted into college. If we do well in college, we will find a rewarding job. The death of a baby reminds us in a very dramatic way that outcomes do not always represent actions. In her unit called Traumatic Loss and Grief Dr. Gilbert states "Traumatic losses confront what appears to be a basic belief of our Western culture that present the world as fair and just. The loss that is unfair or unjust can only be described as a loss of balance between the linked processes of action and result in their lives." Tim and Jenn kept saying "But we did everything right." They most certainly did. Jenn had a checkup before she became pregnant. They researched and talked about their beliefs regarding pregnancy and birth before they chose their care providers. They went to a holistic center where they were very involved in every aspect of Jenn's prenatal care. They were extremely conscientious about nutrition and environmental influences. They had certified nurse midwives attending the labor. And their beloved, much wanted daughter died. This threatened to shatter my deeply held beliefs about childbirth. I had been extremely involved in the natural childbirth movement. I had advocated for and testified at health department hearings for third party reimbursement for certified nurse midwives. I taught prepared childbirth classes for many years. I have personal biases against the casual use of medication in labor and unwarranted medical interventions. I am adamantly pro-breast feeding. I was thrilled when Jenn told me where she was receiving prenatal care. I struggled with the perceived conflict between what I had believed in for so many years and the outcome of my granddaughter's birth. Finally I admitted that our sense of control is illusory. Life is not predictable. There are no guarantees. I have not lost my faith in the birth process, but I have an increased awareness that all the planning in the world can't guarantee the desired outcome. Susan Hendricks wrote a guest column for Tom Golden's web site Crisis, Grief & Healing about her family's grief journey following the death of her daughter. She says "What has changed most is our world view and our spirituality. The belief that good things happen to good people is gone forever and has been replaced with the sense that anytime, anywhere, irrespective of our actions or good intentions, the absurd can break into our lives."

For me, as well as many others, one of the keys to releasing the pain is to talk. The need to talk about the experience over and over is great. It's as though by repeating every detail we are searing it into our memory. Unfortunately, this need may continue on much longer than friends think it should. I found myself apologizing constantly. I also couldn't remember what I had told one person and what I hadn't. So then I apologized for that. I felt as though I was burdening my friends because I couldn't stop talking about Maddy. It is ironic that if I were repeating myself in telling about Maddy's red eyebrows or her first smile, I wouldn't have felt the need to apologize. It is acceptable to babble on excitedly about joyous events, but considered dwelling to talk about the circumstances of our grandchild's death. These too few stories are the only memories we have.

> Journal entry:
> When somebody asks "Do you mind talking about it?" my mental response is "Are you kidding? That's all I want to talk about!" I am consumed with thoughts of Maddy. I don't want to talk about anything else but Maddy. My grief is the only reality I know.

Months after Maddy died I still felt somewhat disconnected from everyday conversations and events. I could only be attentive up to a point, and then I just lost interest. I was surprised that nobody seemed to notice that I was fading away. Based on the depth and intensity of my emotional reactions, I couldn't believe that there was no outward indication of the severity of my suffering. The first few weeks, when people asked how I was doing, I told them quite honestly that I was not doing well at all. After awhile, I sensed that people really didn't want to hear that I was still in pain, so I just shrugged and said I was okay. In his book *Swallowed by a Snake: The Gift of the Masculine Side of Healing*, Tom Golden says "Our culture is not a safe place to grieve. With the massive denial of death that occurs, there is a resulting disdain for grief. Both men and women are forced into a situation where their grief is not honored by the culture or the people around them." Many people seem to assign an arbitrary time frame to how long it should take us to get back to normal. The definition of normal is forever changed for bereaved grandparents. We will never return to exactly the life we knew before our grandchild died. We will never be quite the same person. There will always be a sense of something missing. This is not to say that we will never know happiness or joy again. Eventually we will reach a point where thoughts and emotions even out. We must find a new normal, one that permits us to acknowledge and honor our beloved grandchild. Not only do we need to redefine our world, we may well have to redefine ourselves. During the pregnancy we began to self-identify as a grandparent. Friends and co-workers may have teasingly started calling us Grandma. Now we struggle with the challenge of what to do with that part of our identity, especially if this was our first grandchild. Ethan's grandmother, Nancy, writes "I always dread the question "And how many grandchildren do you have?" I of course answer one. I have had people try to discount that I even am a grandmother. Of course I am a grandmother. I will always be a grandmother."

Grief seems to come over us in waves. Many experts who have studied the grieving process extensively believe that bereaved people experience the worst of their grief about six months after the loss. The initial reaction of shock and numbness quickly gives way to openly visible expressions of sadness. Then people seem to experience a plateau, when they return to work and socializing. Gradually, the cards and phone calls slow down. When the next wave of grief hits, it is frequently unexpected. I had read about the grief process and yet I was still unprepared. This part of the grief journey feels like falling off a cliff. There is no safety net to break the fall. I felt as though I were walking backward on my grief journey. The full impact of my loss hit without warning. I found it incredibly difficult to see a baby, or hear about a co-worker giving birth or becoming a grandparent. At first, it was only newborn babies that I avoided. After several months

I found it difficult to see older babies or even toddlers, especially girls. I feared that I was never going to recover from the tragedy of Maddy's death. Every time I saw a little girl all I could think of was what I was missing. It helped me tremendously when a counselor pointed out that I was not going backwards, I was entering the next phase. I was beginning to realize the enormity of what I had lost.

Journal entry:
> Today I saw a man with a red headed baby. The baby was in a backpack and appeared to be about 9 months old. I couldn't tell if it was a boy or a girl. The hair was bright golden red, the color of Tim's, the color I imagine Maddy's might have been. When I see babies, especially girls, I usually avert my eyes, but I couldn't stop staring at this baby. It is almost as though I needed to feel the pain, to check and be sure it still hurts. And oh how it hurts. Pain is not the constant companion it was at first, but it is just as wrenching.

The change of seasons can be difficult if expectations for the significance of the time of year aren't met. Kathy, Maddy's maternal grandmother, was distressed when the first hints of spring left her feeling worse rather than better. She had believed that the nicer weather would help to lift her heavy feelings. Instead the pleasant days reminded her of the hopes and plans she had for the first spring with her grandchild. She was forced to confront the loss of those dreams.

Holidays are often unbearable. Thanksgiving has always been my favorite holiday, and as the fall progressed I fervently hoped that Jenn would deliver on time. Tim and Jenn had informed my family that if they delivered by Thanksgiving, they would not want to bring a brand new infant out, and my mother and I had formulated plans to prepare platters after our family gathering and take them over so that there could still be the experience of family. Maddy was born still exactly two weeks before Thanksgiving, and as it turned out this was the first time I didn't see my oldest son and his family either. The holiday that had always been my most cherished, especially in recent years as our family had grown was a nearly silent event. That Christmas was also awkward and painful, with the constant overlay of the loss. Jenn's mother and I struggled to maintain some of the family rituals. We had each already bought many Christmas presents for the baby. Kathy donated the toys she had purchased to charity, which gave her a small sense of comfort. I was unable to even look at the things I had put away for my new grandchild. I have two other grandchildren and needed to find a balance between actively mourning Maddy and trying to maintain some sense of the holiday season for them. I had to force myself to complete my holiday shopping. I was unable to find any joy the first Christmas-it was simply too soon. Easter passed, and I longingly gazed at the tiny dress and pinafore I had made for my granddaughter Kristyn's first Easter, when she was just six weeks old. As the 4th of July approached, I found myself remembering the prior year. I had joined my older son and his family to watch the fireworks. Tim and Jenn were there as well. Tim had his niece, Kristyn, on his shoulders, and I was overcome with joy thinking that the following 4th of July he would have his own baby. Holidays and special family occasions such as birthdays will never be the same. They will forever be colored with the sense of someone missing.

Bereaved families talk about the Year of Firsts. The first holiday, the first spring, what should have been the baby's first birthday. Our year of firsts started with Thanksgiving, a mere two weeks after Maddy's stillbirth. I was too numb to feel anything. I was unable to get any pleasure out of Christmas. A few weeks would pass without a significant first, and then I would get hit all over again. There are so many occasions other than holidays that constitute a first. I can still hear the excitement in Tim's voice the evening he called to tell me of Jenn's pregnancy, and the amazement in Jenn's voice when she told me she had felt the baby move. I can clearly see Tim and Jenn glowing with pride when they presented me with a framed ultrasound picture. They had a wedding anniversary, and I couldn't find a card that didn't gush with the word happy, so I designed one on my computer. Mother's Day and Father's Day were unbearable-I wanted so much to do something, to create a ritual, to acknowledge that my son and daughter-in-law were parents. They did not want any recognition-they spent each of those days alone together, not even talking to other family members on the phone. I had moments of resentment over the fact that they couldn't seem to understand how much I needed to be with them. I didn't know how to reach them through my pain. I didn't know how to convey the depth of my anguish. I wanted to respect their grief and their strength in one another, yet I also needed to spend time with them to help me with my grief. I couldn't seem to find a balance. Quickly, too quickly, the months flew by, and as the first anniversary of Maddy's death approached I felt my anxiety increasing. Not only did we face the major winter holidays of Thanksgiving, Hanukkah and Christmas, but Maddy's maternal grandmother and I both have birthdays a few weeks after her-we had teased each other throughout the pregnancy about the possibility of Jenn delivering on one of our birthdays. Maddy, however, chose to make her entrance a few days before her official due date, exhibiting an independent, stubborn streak inherited in equal measure from her mother and father. In what should have been an extraordinarily joyous coincidence, she was born on her maternal great grandmother's birthday, whose name she carries. Dr. Ellen Zinner writes in an article for the Hospice Foundation's newsletter, Journeys, "A year is the period of a planet's revolution around the sun; three hundred and sixty five days for the earth, longer for some planets, shorter for others. In the life of a bereaved individual, the time period of a year is a relative thing. On the one hand, survivors often are amazed that so much time has passed since the death. Four seasons weathered; the holiday periods endured. It seems impossible that they have borne the pain for a full twelve months. On the other hand, it may seem that time has not moved at all. Emotions and memories seem fresh."

The first anniversary of the baby's death is a day of contradictions. There is the ever-present element of resentment and sadness-we should be helping our children plan a birthday party. I still struggle with what to call this day. I alternately say Maddy's birthday or the anniversary of her birth. Many parents and grandparents use the phrase angel day. We also want to celebrate the precious life of our grandchild. We want to remember and honor our grandchild, as well as reassure our child that their child holds a special place in the family. My friend Wilma and her daughter had a balloon release for Jackson. They wrote messages and attached them to the balloons. Pat, whose granddaughter Brigid died of SIDS, says "We celebrate her birthday by sending balloons up to her. Her twin sister, Isabella, lets them go up and has an identical bunch to keep for herself." Wilma also decorated the tree she planted for her grandson. Other grandmothers told me they wrote their grandchild's name on a balloon before they released it. Beryle organized a teddy bear drive to complement the one her daughter and son-in-law were having across the country. Beryle collects teddy bears, so this activity was especially meaningful to her. Jenn's mother had taken a stained glass class, and she made a gorgeous hanging dragonfly. I made wall hangings for people. I found several different fabrics with dragonflies on them and created each wall hanging in a different design. I have heard grandparents say that the first anniversary of the baby's death has all the symbolism of the New Year. It is an opportunity to reflect on the past year. It is also a chance to consciously declare our intention to engage in living, and to recognize that this experience has indeed changed us.

I received an issue of the AGAST newsletter during the first holiday season after Maddy's stillbirth and found the resolutions listed below. I have had this on the bulletin board over my desk at work since then, as a reminder to myself that my feelings are normal, my reactions are healthy, and I am entitled to my grief.

New Year's Resolutions for Bereaved Grandparents
Adapted from "New Year's Resolutions for Bereaved Parents"

By Nancy A. Mower, The Compassionate Friends

I RESOLVE:

- To grieve as much and for as long as I feel like grieving; I will not let others put a timetable on my grief

- To grieve in whatever way I feel like grieving; I will ignore those who try to tell me what I should or should not be feeling and how I should or should not be behaving

- To cry whenever and wherever I feel like crying; I will not hold back my tears just because someone else feels I should be "brave" or "getting better" or "healing by now"

- To talk about my grandchild as often as I want to; I will not let others turn me off just because they can't deal with their own feelings

- That I will not expect family and friends to know how I feel, understanding that someone who has not lost a grandchild cannot possibly know how it feels

- Not to blame myself for my grandchild's death; I will remind myself that feelings of guilt are a normal part of the grieving process, and they will pass

- That I will not be afraid or ashamed to seek professional help if it is necessary

- To commune with my grandchild at least once a day in whatever way feels comfortable and natural to me; I will not feel compelled to explain this communion to others or to justify, or even discuss it with them

- To try to eat, sleep and exercise every day in order to give my body the strength it needs to help me cope with my grief

- To know that I am not losing my mind; I will remind myself that loss of memory, feelings of disorientation, lack of energy and a sense of vulnerability are all normal parts of the grief process

- To know that I will heal, even though it will take a long time

- To let myself heal and not feel guilty about feeling better

- To remind myself that the grief process is circuitous and I will not make steady upward progress; when I find myself slipping back into the old moods of despair and depression I will tell myself that "slipping backward" is also a normal part of the grief process and these moods, too, will pass

- To try to be happy about something for some part of every day, knowing that at first I may have to force myself to think cheerful thoughts so that eventually they can become a habit

- To reach out at times to help someone else, knowing that helping others will help me to get over my depression

- That even though my grandchild is dead, I will opt for life, knowing that is what my grandchild would want me to do

CHAPTER 4

THE MANY ROLES OF GRANDPARENTS

It is as grandmothers that our mothers come into the fullness of their grace. When a man's mother holds his child in her gladden arms he is aware of the roundness of life's cycle; of the mystic harmony of life's ways.

Christopher Morley

Grandparents have a much broader role today than traditionally. In many cases, today's grandparents are more actively involved with their grandchildren than those of past generations. The stereotype of grandparents is almost a caricature-the grandmother baking cookies while the grandfather gives piggy back rides and tells stories. In this stereotype, our adult children bring our grandchildren to us for infrequent visits on holidays. This scenario is not reality for the majority of grandparents. Some of us are actually raising our grandchildren. Many of us care for our grandchildren while their parents work, thus relieving our children of the astronomical burden of paying for and finding trustworthy childcare. We travel with our grandchildren-there are actually cruise lines and tour packages designed specifically for "grand-families." Schools have Grandparent's Day. In many instances, it is the grandparent who is present at the school assembly program because the parents are unable to leave work. We attend our grandchildren's sports events and after school activities. We do things with our grandchildren that we hope will give them a sense of who we are as people. Grandparents today have a much more intimate relationship with their grandchildren than past generations of grandparents. Theater has always been a significant part of my life. As soon as my grandchildren were old enough I started buying season tickets to attend the local children's theater. The afternoons we go to the plays are very special times. I am always cognizant of the fact that I am creating lasting memories. When I learned that my youngest son and his wife were pregnant, I looked at a calendar and figured out the year in which I could start taking their child to the plays.

Our grandchildren are our future. We are heavily invested in these hopes and dreams, and when the eagerly awaited baby dies, so do the hopes and dreams. Our children and grandchildren are our immortality. This is true in a much broader sense than carrying on the family name. Many of us derive pleasure and comfort from knowing that we are passing down our values and beliefs as well as the family history. There is the general sense that because we aren't responsible for the day to day details of raising them, we can relax and concentrate on showing our world to our grandchildren in a way we may not have been able to do with our children. Many of us have a greater degree of financial security now than we did when we were young, and we are able to provide our grandchildren with experiences we couldn't afford for our children. We do these things with hearts overflowing with love and joy.

How well do parents and children, especially adult children, really know one another? Do parents ever see their children as separate adults with their own hopes and dreams? Do children ever see their parents as people? All of these thoughts were things I questioned in the first days and weeks after Maddy's birth. As I talked with my daughter-in-law, I came to know my son better than in all the years I spent raising him. I actually felt guilty because I hadn't completely seen the fine man he had become. Certainly, I was proud of him, and I was sincere in my praise of the solid life he was building with his wife. As I wept over the fact that there was so much about my son I didn't know, I started thinking that there were also many things about me of which he wasn't aware. I agonized over every day that I hadn't called my son to say hello. I had prided myself on not being an interfering mother-in-law. Did he realize that I was trying to show respect for his adulthood and status as a husband by not calling or visiting every day? Now I worried that he might think I wasn't excited about his baby. Even worse, I agonized over whether he thought I didn't care about him.

I learned even more about my son when I heard the remarks he made at Maddy's memorial service. My daughter-in-law also shared with me a letter my son had written to the nurses and midwives who had cared for them during the pregnancy, labor and delivery. I cannot describe the hurt I felt when I read his statement "You are the only ones who truly feel our pain." That statement prompted me to write a letter to my son. In this letter, I shared the many similarities between his feelings during his wife's pregnancy and mine during my pregnancy with him.

Many times over the years I have engaged in conversations regarding the variety of roles that women are expected to fulfill. As I reflected on the incongruence of my role as a bereaved grandmother to that of being a source of strength and support to my son, I again thought of the many roles I play in life. I am a mother. I am a daughter and a sister. I am a grandmother. I am a friend. I am a healthcare professional. In these roles I do my best to fulfill personal, familial and societal expectations. However, I am also an individual with my own accumulated joys and sorrows, hopes and dreams, and past life experiences that influence my manner of reacting and coping.

I came of age during that most magical and wondrous of times, the sixties. I was, and still am, a focused, motivated person. Books and music were my world. I have often used the words of others, especially song lyrics, to give voice to emotions too intense to articulate. The motto of my generation was turn on, tune in and drop out. I got turned on, not to mind-altering substances, but to social activism. I wrote and spoke passionately about the things I believed in. I avidly followed the political and social environment, and I vowed to try and make a difference in the world. I deeply mourned the drug-related deaths of my favorite musicians, listening to their songs over and over and grieving for what works of genius died with them. I did not, however, romanticize them or their drug use. At some level I was angry that they had wasted an extraordinary gift. Although I was adamant in protesting the war in Vietnam, I did not vilify the people who served in the military. Dropping out of school was not an option I ever considered. I wanted to learn everything I could, I devoured the words of others day and night; I had an unquenchable thirst for knowledge and understanding and tolerance. I truly believed that peace love and flowers was the answer to the problems of society. I could always find the silver lining behind each cloud. I was a generally optimistic person who saw life as a grand adventure, something to eagerly participate in rather than something which happened to me. I threw myself into each new experience with a true passion.

I entered my twenties, married and planned a family. Becoming involved in the natural childbirth movement was a perfect segue for me. Once again I had a mission; I had a purpose. I studied and read and attended workshops and volunteered as a lactation consultant, offering advice and support to breast-feeding mothers. I took a training course to become a prepared childbirth instructor. I thrived in this environment of women who believed that pregnancy and childbirth were normal, natural functions. I was thoroughly enmeshed in this culture for close to ten years. I saw so many positive changes come about as a result of the writing and advocacy within this group. The importance of bonding with a newborn baby became widely recognized. Family centered birth experiences became the norm. Couples were encouraged to be actively involved in making a birth plan, and doctors listened to them-the phrase family centered maternity care entered the obstetrical lexicon. Fathers were widely accepted in the delivery room. We researched and wrote position papers and developed protocols that permitted fathers to be in attendance during a cesarean delivery. We read the early literature disputing the absolute necessity for repeat cesareans, and I co-wrote a curriculum for couples interested in a vaginal delivery after a prior cesarean. We argued that the phrase cesarean section was demeaning-grapefruits are sectioned, women give birth- and successfully changed the terminology to cesarean birth or delivery. These activities reinforced my idealistic teenage beliefs that advocacy could effect purposeful change.

The HIV epidemic once again found me firmly entrenched in social activism. I was counseling and working with groups of people facing great stigma on many levels. My voice has been loud and insistent when it comes to public health policies and lack of federal funding that disenfranchises the people I care for even further. I have published and spoken, both locally and nationally, on many psychosocial issues related to living with HIV. My life, both personal and professional, has been spent trying to make things better for others. I have devoted my life to advocating for constructive change. Yet with my granddaughter's stillbirth I am faced with something I can't make better. There is no silver lining behind this cloud. I have spent my entire career helping other people and I can't help my own son. This has been a major stumbling block for me. As time passed, I realized that I needed to take a broader view of how to help my son. I can't ease his pain, but I can make sure that people know he is a father who had a daughter named Maddy. I can't make the fact of Maddy's death better, but hopefully, through my words, I can demonstrate her significance.

Another role that may present conflict for a grandparent is that of profession. A source of stress that was rapidly depleting my minimal store of emotional energy was my effort to interact with my family on a professional level. An acquaintance that is a hospice nurse advised me that I could not be my family's bereavement counselor. Nor could I be my own. One of the most difficult things I've ever done in my life was to see a therapist for personal bereavement counseling. The day I talked to her and asked if she would see me as a patient was the first time in my life I have ever said out loud to another person "I can't do this." (My mother will undoubtedly be quick to announce that it was not the first time I said "I won't do this") As many people working in psychosocial supportive services, I am reluctant to ask for help for myself. I will advocate endlessly for my family, friends and patients, while not recognizing or acknowledging my own needs. Dr. Earl Grollman is a writer, lecturer and rabbi who has written many books and articles on coping with loss. In an interview published on the Hospice Foundation of America's web site, he refers to the issue I've just described as professional hypocrisy. He defines this as "dispensing counsel to others about leading a balanced life and ignoring this advice for ourselves. Our training as often autonomous decision-makers frequently translates into denying our own need for help." He goes on to say, "Because of our professional background, we are expected to "handle" whatever comes along. Clergy members and professionals need to know that they have a right to grieve- it is not a sign of weakness but a sign of strength. And they must also give themselves permission to not be in charge." He discusses the fact that when his mother died, he was able to articulate that his role in her funeral would be that of a grieving son, not a rabbi conducting the service. This applies to our workplace community as well as our family. A common saying among the legal profession is that a lawyer who represents himself has a fool for a client. It can be very difficult to disassociate from our professional role as a caregiver or counselor, yet it is this very separation that allows our needs for comfort and support to be met. It is equally difficult to separate ourselves from others' perceptions of us as the all-knowing parent. A large part of my internal struggle was that so much of my self- identity was shattered when Maddy died. If part of my role as a mother is to protect my child, then I had failed miserably. My identity as a grandmother has also been altered-there is no baby to brag about or show off. A standard counseling technique is to have people explore and identify the skills or activities that have previously helped them to cope successfully with major traumatic life events. My identity as a competent healthcare professional had been a source of resilience in the past, and now I needed to step away from this role. I needed to consciously give up control at a time in my life when so much control had been removed already.

One of my dearest friends is a social worker who worked for a hospice organization for many years. On the one-month anniversary of Maddy's stillbirth I e-mailed him the following:

> I'm having a tough time. It's really hard for me to admit this. I'm the one who has always been strong and tough and taken care of everybody. I'm supposed to be the counselor. Today is one month-it doesn't seem possible. How could it be a month already?

I printed his response and carried it in both my briefcase and my purse, reading it so often I had to print out new copies. His words still comfort me.

Just remember that although you're strong, you are also human. And just because you're strong, it doesn't give you supernatural powers to avoid very real, human feelings. You are allowed to feel this way. It doesn't mean that you are weak. It means that you are feeling the feelings of a grandmother who just suffered one of the most terrible things that a grandparent can go through. So allow yourself to be okay with feeling this way. Because these feelings are tough enough, without beating yourself up on top of it.

Many of today's grandparents are still working. Policies for bereavement leave vary widely. I was granted one day; fortunately I had other leave time I was able to access. I cannot imagine returning to work after only one day. I was still struggling to focus and concentrate and be productive weeks after Maddy died. I have an extremely supportive environment where I work, and I realize how unusual that is. The genuine compassion and empathy I received (and continue to receive) from my co-workers is the only possible way I could have returned to work. Not all grandparents are as fortunate as I am in this regard. Many times grandparents must return to work so that they can offer their children financial assistance with the unexpected expenses of burying a child. We may go back to work quickly to keep busy, to distance ourselves from the intense feelings of bereavement. This only helps for a limited time-sooner or later we have to face our pain in order to deal with it in a mentally healthy manner. Some of us find the workplace a refuge from our children's pain. Our own pain threatens to overwhelm us, but to see our children in so much pain is, in many cases, more than we can bear. This adds another layer of complicated emotions for grandparents. We want to be able to help our children in any way possible, and yet we have other responsibilities. We are pulled in many different directions. We need to return to work for financial reasons as well as limitations on time off, yet we want to be available to our child. We need to grieve our loss, yet we feel as though we must hold it together and appear strong in front of our children. We want to spend every minute with our bereaved child, yet we may have other family members who also need us.

Even with the extraordinary amount of caring and support I received in my work environment, my return to work was not easy. I work in a large hospital, but my unit is very small. I had a few lectures scheduled, and Pat, my boss, immediately told me she would cover them for me. Five days after Maddy died, Pat's elderly aunt, who had lived with her family for years, died rather unexpectedly. There was a large training scheduled in collaboration with an outside agency, so exactly one week after my granddaughter was stillborn I packed up my laptop and projector and went to give a lecture on HIV. This is a training I do three times a year, I know most of the other people involved, and a very close friend was going to be in attendance, so I thought I could handle it. I was unaware of the fact that the woman who was presenting with me was seven months pregnant. When I saw her I went completely numb. She presented first and I didn't hear a word she said. I don't know how I managed to get through my two hour lecture. This was her first baby, and I sensed that she was extremely uncomfortable seeing me. That was my first inkling that people would find it difficult to be around me. I was visible proof that pregnancy and birth does not always have a joyous outcome.

Grandparents may have difficulty being around their other grandchildren. This discomfort could stem from many different sources. Families might have a preference, whether privately held or openly acknowledged, for gender. It could feel like an added indignity if the baby was the preferred gender. People often will not discuss these feelings. I didn't know the gender of either of my children before they were born. When my second son was born, the doctor actually asked me in the delivery room if I was disappointed. I was thrilled-I wanted boys, although I had never told anybody. When my oldest son's first child was a boy, I didn't have any thoughts of wishing he had been a girl. However, when my daughter-in-law was pregnant the second time, a late ultrasound showed fairly definitively that the baby was a girl. I was amazed at the excitement I felt. I had seen enough inaccurate ultrasound readings in my years of working in the prenatal field that I did not allow myself to believe it until she was born. I must admit that my excitement over a granddaughter was rather superficial-the idea of buying girl clothes after two generations of boy clothes was what appealed to me. The gender issue could be very important in a family with several generations of the same gender.

There are so many facets to the grief carried by grandparents. Our hearts break at the sight of our children's anguish, and we long to help them. At the same time, we are also experiencing what feels like unbearable pain, and we need to find our way through our own grief. As tempting as it is to deny what we are feeling, we cannot put our grief aside while we help our child. It sounds contradictory to say that we need to do our own grieving simultaneously while doing whatever we can to provide comfort for our child, but that is precisely the complexity of being a bereaved grandparent. Kathleen Gilbert says "Faced with a traumatic loss, many (sometimes all) family members will face periods of time when they will be overwhelmed by the loss and its meaning. There will be times when individual family members will need to step back from their participation in family processing of the loss and focus on their own needs. They may simply be overwhelmed by their own pain, unable to maintain their role in the family." Unfortunately, a grandparent's grief may often be overlooked because others see us in our usual context within the family. We are expected to take charge, to take care of our bereaved child, to keep the family unit running smoothly. Our grief is invisible, our tears forgotten.

The Grieving Grandparent as a Parent

Grandparents of my generation serve multiple roles. We are also parents. We are used to fixing the problems our children faced as they grew up. When my son was learning to walk, if he fell down I could pick him up, give him a hug, and stand him back on his feet. When he fell off his bike, I could bandage his scraped knee and send him on his way again. As he made his way through the teenage years, I was there to listen, offer advice, and advocate for my child if need be. I could always do something, always make his situation better. When his daughter died, I was finally confronted with something I couldn't fix. Not only was I unable to fix it, I couldn't even make it better. This was the most powerless I have ever felt in my life. I am Tim's mother and I am supposed to offer him wisdom and solutions. He should be turning to me for answers, and I have none. The only thing I can give my son in this situation is an unconditional and never ending supply of love. Yet somehow, I feel as though I should be able to offer him something more. Carla, whose grandson Braxton died of SIDS, says "I was not only hurting for the grandson that I had lost, I was also hurting for my daughter, and the hardest part was knowing that there was nothing that I could do to make her feel better. I could not kiss the pain away like I could when she was little."

Cheryl and John Cox are the bereaved grandparents of A.J. Cheryl's articulate words express the frustration of knowing there is nothing concrete we can do for our child.

> When children are young, they may be comforted by a parent with gentle hugs and kisses and the promise of "It's going to be all right." When your child loses their child to death, it is NOT all right, and it NEVER will be. Suddenly, you realize that nothing you say or do can make it better. You can only be there when your child wants to talk...if they do. You are expected to be strong yet compassionate; holding her while her body is racked with great heaving sobs, listening quietly as she screams out her rage, watching helplessly as she sits listlessly with that far-off look in her eyes. Over and over these storms of emotion attack your child. It may be the first time in your child's life that she realizes you can do nothing to make things right for her. You pray that God gives her strength to get through these toughest of times. It is a very helpless feeling.

Margaret Gerner is a bereaved grandmother who has written a booklet, *Grief of Grandparents*, available through the web site of the Centering Corporation. In an AGAST article excerpting the opening of her booklet, she describes how she felt after her daughter's baby died:

> I am powerless, I am helpless, I am frustrated, I sit here and cry with her. She cries for her daughter and I cry for mine. I cannot help her. I can't reach inside and take her broken heart. I must watch her suffer day after day and see her desolation. Where is my power now? Where is my mother's bag of tricks that will make it all better? Where are the answers? I should have them. I'm a mother.

I cried as often and as hard for my son as I cried for myself. Knowing the intensity of my pain, I found even the contemplation of the depth of his pain unimaginable. As a mother who had reveled in being pregnant, I could not imagine what my daughter-in-law was experiencing. Jenn's mother and I talked on the phone often, lengthy conversations for the most part consisting of us saying to one another "How are our children going to survive this?" We were extremely concerned about the son and daughter we loved so dearly. It was hard for us not to feel rejected when we called them and they didn't want to talk. Fortunately, we were able to support each other. We look upon the bond and friendship that we formed at this time as a gift from Maddy. Margo says, "There were times when I looked into Stacy's lost dark eyes and thought I would never see the face of my real daughter again. That is what cut my heart to ribbons even more than losing Peyton-the thought that I had lost my daughter as well." The emotions grandparents feel watching their adult child grieve are universal. Mary Lou Reed has worked in both medical and mental health fields, and is an active member of the Association for Death Education and Counseling (ADEC). She is the author of *Grandparents Cry Twice: Help for Bereaved Grandparents.* In an article for ADEC's quarterly journal, she says "The extraordinary emotional and psychological effort grandparents experience trying to cope with a grandchild's death often seems to be a challenge far beyond what most grandparents believe they can endure."

We instinctively want and need to parent our adult children when anything bad happens. For us, taking care of our children is a channel for the joy and love we had for their baby. We may unconsciously step back into our role of making decisions and telling our children not only what they "should" be doing, but also how to do things. There is a consensus among grief researchers that the difficult and overwhelming decisions facing bereaved parents need to be handled by them. In the first quarter 2003 issue of The Forum, ADEC's quarterly journal, the professional development theme was grandparent grief. Tom Easthope, a certified death educator/funeral director writes about the dynamics he sees in the funeral home. "As parents, most of us feel a need to protect our children. This can even apply to adult children when a grandchild dies. It's like a knee-jerk reaction. We want to ease the burden or remove it completely, not realizing the consequences. I have seen many well-intentioned grandparents disenfranchise their children's grief by taking over right from the get go." Parents who have had these decisions made by others often have trouble resolving their grief. Years later they express resentment that not only did they suffer the death of their baby, but choices and arrangements that were made were contrary to their wishes and brought them no comfort.

Many grandparents struggle with stepping back and permitting their adult children to be in charge. This struggle comes from a genuine love and the desire to protect our children from anything painful. As hard as it is, we cannot shield our children from this pain. We would willingly bear the pain for them, but we can't. They need to face their pain head on and develop their own skills for coping and surviving. Think of the many experiences you have had as a parent that have enabled you to step back and allow your child to handle life. You may not realize the full scope of your strong coping skills. The first time you put your child on a school bus, you may have had coffee with other parents as a means of coping with the trauma of letting your child go out into the world alone. How hard it was to allow your son or daughter to drive your car-but you did it, you trusted their ability to make safe decisions about handling a vehicle. When your child left home, whether to go to college or move into an apartment and enter the work world, you hoped and prayed that he or she would act responsibly. Now even more than ever, you need to give your child the opportunity to make decisions. Provide a warm, supportive environment and be willing to listen and accept the choices your child makes. If your son or daughter wants something very different from what you believe in, remind yourself that this may not be the first time you have disagreed with a decision your child has made. This is an opportunity to truly show our children the meaning of unconditional love. The only way your child will be able to grieve productively and eventually heal is if you allow him to do it his own way.

This does not mean that grandparents should not be involved in the decisions and arrangements surrounding the death of their grandchild. Unfortunately, there are decisions that need to be made quickly. There are almost always options, and grandparents can ask questions and help to clarify details. This is a time when nobody is thinking clearly, when it seems impossible to face what has happened, and we are being asked to make decisions about things we've never remotely considered. Many decisions don't have to be made immediately, and we can encourage our children to only deal with the ones that absolutely have to be made at the moment. We can provide guidance and support. Because of my professional experiences and my connections in the community, my son and daughter-in-law turned to me when the midwife asked them which funeral home they wanted to use. I know many of the employees at the funeral home I recommended, and I knew they would attend to my family's needs with sensitivity and empathy. This was certainly not among the many gifts I had planned for my grandchild, and yet it did make me feel useful. It also gave me a measure of comfort to know that the people involved in Maddy's memorial service were people who know me personally. It helped to fulfill my need to do something.

We can help our children in practical ways that don't interfere with their needs and wishes, but allow us to fulfill our desire to help. I accompanied my son and daughter-in-law to the funeral home, but respected their need to make all of the arrangements for the service by themselves, while I waited in the lobby. The anguish in my daughter-in-law's sobs was piercing. How unfair, I thought. I should be consulting with a financial planner over opening a college fund, not choosing memorial cards with a funeral director. When they asked the funeral director if they could see and hold their baby one more time, they also asked if I would like to see her again. My daughter-in-law's parents were with us that day, and this was their first and only opportunity to see their beloved granddaughter. This request was handled with much respect and dignity. The funeral director dressed Maddy in an outfit my son and daughter-in-law had brought with them, and arranged her on blankets they had also brought. Jenn's parents and I went in to see and touch her first. We told her how much we wanted and loved her, we assured her that she would always be a part of us, and the two grandmothers told her simultaneously that we would take care of her mommy and daddy. My son and daughter-in-law then had time alone with her, as it was very important to them that they be the last ones to see Maddy.

Grandparents who were not present at the birth need to know that they can see the baby if they wish. It may not even occur to our children to ask us if we would like to see the baby. Our children may not realize how important this is to us. Having an opportunity to see and hold the baby will help us with our grieving process. It also allows us to bear witness to this child we were so eagerly anticipating. It is a way of creating memories that we can share as a family. My granddaughter looked so much like her father, my son. Her silky hair was dark but she had red eyebrows and eyelashes. I noticed that immediately. I can validate back to my son and daughter-in-law how pretty Maddy was. Seeing and holding the baby gives grandparents a chance to say hello and goodbye. It helps our children to see the love we have for their baby. It reassures them of the place their baby has in their extended family.

Family dynamics are as complicated as they are fascinating. Siblings of the bereaved parent might feel that they are being ignored. They may even revert to the old childhood game of "you always loved my brother more." If siblings are estranged, a grandparent may feel a responsibility to intervene and try to facilitate reconciliation. Mary Lou Reed talks about this in her article. She says "The grandparents are then put into the situation of being mediators for a family in grief- to be the peacemakers. What incredible demands the family may place on the already stretched physical, mental, emotional, and psychological strengths of the grandparents!" Our other children, who may be used to seeing us take charge and solve problems in other situations, don't understand how paralyzing our grief is. They don't realize that there is a very good chance we won't even remember a conversation we had with them just the day before. They could be expected to perform within the family in the role that normally would be ours, especially in the logistics of the day of the funeral

Surviving Grandchildren

Surviving grandchildren tend to be ignored when there is a tragedy of this magnitude. We are paralyzed by our grief, barely able to care for ourselves, which may make us emotionally unavailable. Many young children's only knowledge of death comes from watching cartoons on television and playing video games. The supposedly dead character jumps back up, negating the finality of death. Explaining death to children is always difficult, but explaining a death that even adults don't understand is close to impossible. It is appropriate to tell your grandchild that there are some questions for which there are no answers. Young children may be frightened and need assurance that because the baby died doesn't mean they are going to die also. They may also need to be reassured that nothing they thought, said, or did caused the baby's death. Most funeral directors offer counseling services that include the entire family. Compassionate Friends and hospice groups have excellent resources if you are unsure what to say or how to discuss the death with your grandchildren. Alan Wolfelt's web site, Center for Loss & Life Transition, is also a good resource. The consensus among grief counselors and child psychologists is that young children should be given brief, direct answers to questions. If they need more information, they will then ask another question. Rabbi Earl Grollman suggests that rather than talking about heaven or an afterlife, we concentrate on the present and help children to identify their emotions. Children are grounded in the here and now. Children also tend to be much more aware of circumstances than we suspect. I wasn't sure how much my granddaughter Kristyn, who was six, understood about death in general and Maddy's stillbirth. Her comprehension was revealed when she asked if Uncle Tim and Aunt Jenn hated her because she was alive and their baby wasn't.

A potential area of conflict for families could be having children in attendance at the funeral. It can be quite uncomfortable if the bereaved parents feel differently than the children's parents or even the children. As difficult as these conversations are, the bereaved parents should be asked about their feelings before discussing the funeral with other children. Just as you need to permit your bereaved child to make his or her own decisions and plans regarding the service, so do you need to respect the wishes and decisions made by the parents of your surviving grandchildren. A child should never be forced to attend the funeral, nor should he be made to feel guilty if he doesn't want to be present. If the child wants to be there, he should be told what to expect. Describe the setting, including the casket or urn, and let him know that he will see people crying. Ideally, an adult who is close to the child should sit with him and be willing to explain things and answer questions. Many times extended family is not available, and the adults are too incapacitated by their own grief to provide comfort to the child. The large number of people attending the service may overwhelm a child. If the child does not attend the funeral or memorial service, he can be included in a ritual activity at home or at the cemetery at a later date. This enables him to say goodbye in a safe environment, where adults are able to provide understanding and support.

Children, even very young children, grieve. They know something is different in the family. They may not express their grief outwardly. A typical pattern will be for a child to verbalize that it is sad that the baby died, and then run back outside to play with friends. It is important that we remember to reassure our surviving grandchildren that while we are indeed quite sad that the baby died, we love them and are happy that they are alive.

Grandparents' reactions to surviving grandchildren are varied. Some grandparents want to spend more time with their grandchildren, drawing comfort from the hugs and love. They may be able to lose themselves briefly in the joy of concentrating on providing special time with their grandchildren. Other grandparents have shared that it was very difficult to be around their surviving grandchildren. There is a constant feeling of someone missing. Each family situation is different, of course, and those differences may have an impact on how we relate to surviving grandchildren. If they are the children of our bereaved child, we might be expected to care for them during the first days or weeks after the baby's death. Again, providing this care may comfort some grandparents, knowing they are helping their grieving child, while others may be so depleted physically and emotionally that they cannot help in this way. Many grandmothers express difficulty in showing joy for another child's pregnancy. They feel conflicted and guilty. Relationships between siblings may be strained if the pregnancies were during the same time frame. My emotions were midway between the extremes. I live near my oldest son's family, and I am a very involved grandmother. I wanted to see my grandchildren and be with them, but I felt emotionally distant. The first few activities we enjoyed together after Maddy's death were bittersweet to me. I couldn't shake the sense of absence in my life. It took many months for me to engage emotionally with my grandchildren and enjoy them without the overlay of grief for Maddy coming between us. We love our surviving grandchildren and want to spend time with them, but at the same time we feel as though they are being cheated because we are not the same joyful grandparent we once were. There is always the overriding sense that someone is missing. Our other children likely don't understand and may resent that we seem to have withdrawn from their children.

The Grieving Grandparent as a Son/Daughter Great Grandparents

Many grandparents are lucky enough to have their own parents still living. As our parents age we feel a need to protect and care for them, just as we do our children. Today's grandparents are often called the sandwich generation. I felt overwhelmed by the perceived notion that I needed to be emotionally supportive and protective of my parents as well as my adult children. I felt as though I was bearing the weight of the grief of three generations. I wanted to shield my parents from my pain. Just as I wanted to take care of my son, my mother wanted to take care of me. And just as my son needed to find his own way through his grief, I needed to experience my grief. I resented every comment, implied or real, that I needed to be strong for my son. I didn't feel strong; I didn't want to be strong. I wanted to sob and rage at the injustice and mourn openly. I needed for somebody to give me permission to do so. I craved validation of my emotions and recognition for the enormity of my loss.

When it comes to death and grieving, cultural diversity transcends ethnic, religious or racial boundaries. Just as the religious culture a person was raised in gives a template for defining how we should conduct ourselves, so does the era in which a person grew up. Some great-grandparents may have grown up in a time when death was not discussed, or when men were not encouraged to cry. It is likely that they were raised in a time when babies and young children commonly died, so their attitude might differ from ours in several ways. If they grew up in a family where babies died and other children were born and the baby was never talked about, then they may find it very difficult to understand the importance of seeing and holding the baby. They may express discomfort at looking at pictures of the baby. They might even verbalize the cliché "Oh they're young, they'll have another baby." Grandparents could find themselves in the position of running interference between a generation that believes that being strong means not talking about the baby, and another generation that craves assurance that their baby will not be forgotten.

Great grandparents have most likely experienced many deaths over the years. They are living testament to the fact that we can and will survive. Their attitude, however, may seem matter of fact to us. We may find ourselves becoming easily frustrated with our parents, the very people to whom we should be turning for support. In their eagerness to offer us reassurance that our child will find joy again, they may become impatient with our grieving. Their expectations for how we should be handling our grief put even more pressure on us.

CHAPTER 5

COPING

If you suppress grief too much, it can well redouble

Moliere

At the time it occurs, we believe we will never be able to cope with the death of a baby. There are, however, many things that grandparents can do to help themselves and their bereaved children. The ideas and suggestions in this chapter come not only from recommendations of professional bereavement counselors, but also from families. Friends and family members may try to tell you or your child what should or shouldn't be done. We are emotionally fragile and vulnerable to the criticism of others at this time, and it only compounds our grief when we feel as though we are being judged for the things we have chosen to do. It is a human tendency at times of severe stress to find decision-making difficult. If in the future you find yourself regretting something you did or didn't do, it may help to tell yourself that you made the best decision you could at that particular time with the information you had available. The most important thing is to engage in activities that give you comfort and nobody but you will know what those things are. It helps immensely to draw on a support system of family and friends whose only motivation is to love, listen, and be there for you without offering unsolicited advice.

This is a difficult time for the entire family, and the needs and viewpoints of various family members can be quite different. There may be things that are very important to the parents of your grandchild that make you uncomfortable. It is certainly possible that the grandparents or the great grandparents have wishes or beliefs that are contrary to what the parents' desire. Following are a few basic questions that may be useful in determining how forceful you want to be about a particular coping activity. In the long run, is it really going to matter if this was or was not done? Is it important enough to you to impede your own grief journey? Finally, is there a possibility of compromise, or is there a way that you could do this just for yourself if your children are adamant that they do not want to be involved in or include this activity? Not only do grandparents need to be careful about supporting our children's wishes, but we also need to be mindful of each other. The last thing any family needs at a time like this is anger and resentment between family members. Nowhere is this played out more openly than in the arrangements for the funeral or memorial service. Many families today are inter-faith, and religions have markedly different customs and beliefs regarding infant death. In many cases the differences may go far beyond different religious affiliations; there may be family members who are adamantly opposed to any kind of religious service. This may be difficult for some family members to accept. It is possible to have a meaningful ceremony with ritual expressions not conducted by clergy if that is what the parents desire.

For the sake of coherence and organization I am going to discuss various options and suggestions by chronological categories.

At the Time of Delivery

Every situation leading to a baby's death is different. Sometimes it is known or suspected before labor begins that the baby is no longer living. In some cases something goes terribly wrong during labor, resulting in an emergency situation. Perhaps the baby is born with serious medical problems. This may result in the baby being transferred to another facility, forcing the father to choose between staying with his partner and going with the baby. If a grandparent is present or nearby, he or she could stay with the mother so that the father can accompany his baby. Infrequently, there is no indication during labor that the baby is not going to survive, and the stillbirth is totally unexpected, leaving the medical staff attending the birth as stunned as the parents. Family members may not be in attendance at the birth, and parents could be in a position of facing agonizing decisions by themselves. Unfortunately, there are some decisions that need to be made at the time the baby dies. Parents in these situations are in shock and may make a quick decision which they or other family members question or regret at a later time. Grandparents can play a vital supportive role by accepting the decisions their children made under overwhelming circumstances. Parents will usually be asked if they wish to have the baby baptized. They will be asked to consent to an autopsy to determine the cause of death. It is crucial for parents to know that they do not have to respond immediately to this request. They can tell the person asking them to consent that they need to talk about it and perhaps get more information. Parents can hold their baby, and if other family members are present they may also hold the baby. Some parents want to bathe and dress the baby themselves. You can take pictures. I am the family photographer-it's one of the hobbies I take seriously. I had carried my camera in the car the last few weeks of Jenn's pregnancy. As overwhelmed and in shock as I was, I still tried to be respectful of Tim and Jenn and I asked them if they minded if I took pictures of Maddy. At first, Tim was reluctant, but he has since expressed how glad he is to have pictures of his daughter. My son had the presence of mind to ask the nurse if she would put Maddy's handprints and footprints in the baby book. I have no idea where he found the strength to make that request. Ask for a snip of the baby's hair. Undo the blanket and clothing and look closely at your baby if you want. Ask the medical staff to leave you alone with your child, as there may be private things that you want to say. Spend as much time as you need. Feel free to rock your baby, and sing a song. These are all healthy, normal things to do.

I will be forever grateful that my son and daughter-in-law were so generous with allowing me to hold Maddy. I carried her around, talking to her, kissing her and telling her how much I love her. I stroked her hair and her face and memorized every detail. One of my first reactions was a sense of guilt that Jenn's mother was not there-I felt so badly for her, thinking that she would never see or hold her granddaughter. I actually felt guilty because I was there and she wasn't.

If a grandparent is present, he or she may help in making some of the phone calls to other family members and close friends. I cannot begin to describe the agony of calling my mother to tell her that her eagerly anticipated great granddaughter was stillborn. I assumed that she would call my brother, and it wasn't until the next morning that I discovered that she had assumed that I had called him. I reached a point the night Maddy died where I couldn't tell one more person. I couldn't bring myself to say the words one more time. I made only the calls I felt were absolutely necessary, and saved some for the next day.

Funeral/Memorial Service

Although funeral services are designed to honor the deceased, the intention is to provide comfort for the survivors. Social support is crucial, and a service is an excellent way for people to acknowledge the loss and provide that support. In his article *Why is the Funeral Ritual Important?* Dr. Alan Wolfelt writes "We are all social beings whose lives are given meaning in relation to the lives of those around us. The funeral helps us begin this difficult process of developing a new self-identity because it provides a social venue for public acknowledgement of our new roles." There are numerous options available for families. This is an area where family members may well disagree. As difficult as it is for grandparents, they should allow their children to make the decisions. The death of a baby is a stark reminder of how little control we actually have over life events. We think we are shielding our children from even more pain if we arrange everything, but the reality is that by denying them the opportunity of planning a service, we rob our children even further of a sense of control. The parents need to decide whether they want the baby cremated or buried. There are many factors to take into consideration when making this decision. If there is a family plot, it may not be located near where the parents are living. Parents may not be living in a permanent location, and if the baby is buried in a local cemetery they might feel as though they can never move. Cremation allows the option for future burial of the urn if the parents desire to do so. Many parents, because they had so little time with the baby, want and need to bring the urn home. Parents may choose items to place in the casket, or have cremated with the baby. My son had a piece of the monitor tracing strip cremated with Maddy, because he wanted to symbolically give her back her heartbeat. Tim and Jenn also had snips of their hair cremated with Maddy, so she would always have her mommy and daddy with her.

Some parents want a formal funeral or memorial service in a church or funeral home, and others choose to have a service in an outdoor location. Some times the parents want a private ceremony, with a memorial service held at a future date. Incorporating rituals into the service helps family members to begin coping. We had a candle lighting ceremony at the conclusion of Maddy's service. Immediate family lit tapers from a pillar candle that had been burning throughout the ceremony. The tapers then surrounded the pillar. The pillar symbolized Maddy, and to me, the ritual symbolized the family's acknowledgement of Maddy's significance and place within the family. I keep the taper I lit standing next to a framed picture of Maddy.

Caring for Ourselves

The days and weeks following the funeral are often even more difficult than the days leading up to the service. The numbness is wearing off, and we are faced with the realization that the baby really is dead. The visits and phone calls from friends tend to slow down. Attending to the details of the funeral fills the hours for a brief period. As painful as this is, assisting with the arrangements gives us something to do. It is when we are finally alone with our grief that we need to find activities that comfort us. There is no right or wrong to any of this. Each one of us needs to find peace and comfort in our own way, and the activity that is most meaningful to one person may not fit in with another person's needs or beliefs. Not only is it important to accept the needs and wishes of other family members, but we should also be accepting of our own needs in remembering and memorializing our grandchild. Grandparents often ignore their own feelings while they do whatever possible to get their child through the initial nightmare. This makes it easy for others to see us only in our role of supporting and caring for our bereaved child, and overlook our own sorrow. Pushing aside our grief and not acknowledging the impact of the baby's death hinders our ability to heal the pain.

We may feel isolated in our grief, and the intensity of our emotions may be difficult for others to witness. It is important to identify a support system of family and friends who can listen to us and accept the visible signs of our grief. We need to be with others who will permit us to tell our story over and over. Dr. Alan Wolfelt talks about this in an article on the Center for Loss and Life Transition web site: "Reaching out to others and accepting support is often difficult, particularly when you hurt so much. But the most compassionate self-action you can do at this difficult time is to find a support system of caring friends and relatives who will provide the understanding you need. Seek out those people who encourage you to be yourself and acknowledge your feelings-both happy and sad." You may find friendships changing. A woman I had considered a close friend called to express her condolences and told me she wouldn't be at the funeral because she couldn't handle it. My immediate response was one of hurt. How did she think I felt? Did she really think I could handle it? Later, I appreciated the fact that she called and was honest. I still missed seeing her at a time when I desperately needed my friends, but I understood. Consider joining a support group if friends are reluctant to hear about the baby. Other grandparents who have had a grandchild die are the only people who know exactly how we feel. I have found a few online support groups for bereaved grandparents that I've listed in the bibliography. These groups are extremely helpful for many reasons beyond the obvious one of having somebody to talk to. Being online eliminates the excuse of being too tired or not wanting to get dressed and leave the house. You can also go online any time of the day or night, depending on your need to connect, rather than having to wait for a regularly scheduled meeting. Professional counseling can also be of great value; it may well be the only opportunity a grandparent has to focus completely on her own experience and feelings. It can make a tremendous difference to have your feelings validated and to have someone tell you that your thoughts and reactions are normal. A therapist with expertise in bereavement counseling can help you feel comfortable with all of the possible manifestations of grief. There were many weeks when the hour I spent in counseling was the only good time within that week.

Henri Nouwen was a priest who spent two years at the Menninger Clinic doing a fellowship in the religion and psychiatry program, studying the combination of psychology and theology. He wrote more than forty books exploring the spiritual life. His words are lyrical:

> When we honestly ask ourselves which persons in our lives mean the most to us, we often find that it is those who, instead of giving much advice, solutions, or cures, have chosen rather to share our pain and touch our wounds with a gentle and tender hand. The friend who can be silent with us in a moment of despair or confusion, who can stay with us in an hour of grief and bereavement, who can tolerate not knowing, not curing, not healing, and face with us the reality of our powerlessness, that is the friend who cares.

This was what I needed more than anything-the friend who could be silent with me. I didn't want friends to fill the silence; I needed them to share the silence. I didn't really want consolation; I wanted someone to acknowledge the enormity of my loss and validate my right to grieve.

Writing is a creative outlet. Many people find it helpful to write their thoughts in a journal. I have kept a journal for many years, and this was one of the first things I did after Maddy died. I poured out my love and pain, the words spilling from my heart to the paper. I frequently wrote the same thing over and over. My journal doesn't mind when I do that. It doesn't tell me that it's time to put the tragedy behind me and move on. I used some of the earliest journal entries when I was composing my remarks for Maddy's memorial service, and I continue to draw thoughts from my journal for this book. When you are writing privately, just for you, you don't have to worry about saying the right thing; think of journaling as talking to yourself. Let the hurt and anger and frustration out. I have never attempted to censor or edit my journal. I have often felt that it is the one and only place where I can say everything I am thinking and feeling without fear of rejection.

Another writing activity that some people find helpful is to compose letters. These can be kept in a journal or in a three ring binder. You can write letters to your grandchild, your adult child, even your friends. You might even write letters to yourself. Similar to keeping a journal, the letters are not necessarily being written for anybody else to read, unless you choose to share them with your child.

Margo Einsig wrote a very personal letter to her grandson after he was stillborn. She decided to share it in the hopes that it will comfort other grandparents who find themselves caught in this nightmare. Margo explains "I was at the depths of despair when I wrote this-somehow it helped me to bear the pain that cannot be borne. I placed this letter in a sealed envelope in Peyton's "Memory Box."

A letter written to Peyton Michael Hines from his loving Grandmother (Nanna), Margo Einsig, on October 28, 2003 -- 23 days after his Silent Birth.

To Peyton,

My dear little grandson. I want to tell you how very much I love you and miss you. When your Mommy told me that she was going to have a baby, I was the happiest person in the world. You see, I knew how much she and Daddy wanted you and what wonderful parents they would have been to you. They already loved you so much and took such good care of you. Mommy (Stacy) went to all of her doctor appointments, took real good care of her health, did not smoke or drink, ate her fruits and vegetables. Daddy (Mike) helped her and encouraged her and laid his head on her tummy so you could feel him close to you. Your entire family was thrilled to hear that you were on your way. It had been eight years since we had a baby in the family and you were our very first little boy. We waited impatiently and could barely stop ourselves from jumping up and down.

Your Nanna and Aunt Courtney got busy buying baby clothes, soft blankets, diapers and toys. Pop-Pop set out with Mommy to buy your furniture. Great Aunt Catherine started her famous knitting of baby clothes and stuffed toys. Your cousins, Caitlyn and Heather, made plans to baby sit (if Mommy would give you up for a moment), and to play with you and entertain you. Family and friends planned and shopped for your baby shower. What a wonderful, happy day that was. Everyone had so much fun and your Mommy just glowed with happy anticipation and good health.

Finally, with a short time left until your birth, we were <u>so</u> ready for your arrival. Your nursery was all freshly painted in soft baby blue and trimmed out with the cutest snuggle bugs bedding and border. Your crib and dresser were in place along with the "Mommy" chair that Pop-Pop bought so that your Mommy could feed you and rock you gently to sleep. All your cute baby clothes and soft little blankets were waiting for you in your closet and drawers.

Daddy kept busy-checking all the time to make sure that Mommy was healthy and comfortable. He dreamed about his little sports buddy, and spent a lot of time picking the perfect name for you. Some of those up for consideration were Ethan, Tristan and Elijah, but then suddenly he decided on the wonderful name he chose for you "Peyton Michael Hines." We all laughed and said, "Yes, that's it-it's perfect." I hope you know how much he was looking forward to being your Dad. He loves sports and was hoping that he could share that love with you. But, he said, even if you grew up not to be a sports nut like him, he didn't care. He just wanted to enjoy nurturing you and raising you, and helping you become whatever you wanted to be.

I don't have to tell you what a great Mommy you had, 'cause you already know what good care she took of you all those months when you were growing inside her. She did everything she could to make sure that you were born strong and healthy. Remember how she would sit on the sofa-kinda watching TV-but really thinking about you as she gently rubbed her tummy and smiled. Remember how Daddy would put his face down on Mommy's tummy to talk to you and try to listen to your little heartbeat.

Then came the day when all our hopes and dreams vanished. Silently, you were born into this world. Our little Angel. So beautiful and perfect that it broke my heart. How your Mommy and Daddy cried-so sad that they would never take you home to your blue nursery and place you in your comfortable crib. Mommy would never rock you in the "Mommy" chair. Daddy would never play with you and show you off to his friends. Caitlyn and Heather would never baby-sit for you. Aunt Catherine would never see you wear the sweater sets she knitted for you, or to wrap you in the blankets she made, or see you play with the magical animals that she knits and stuffs.

Your Nanna will never again hold you or kiss away your boo-boos, or sing 'Happy Birthday" as you push your little face into your first birthday cake. Mommy and Daddy will never hear your first words or see you take your first steps. Pop-Pop will never swing you into the air on a clear crisp morning as the leaves rustle under his feet. How I long to hold you to my heart and feel your soft baby breath on my cheek. How I long to smell that wonderful clean baby smell as I wrap you in a warm towel, fresh from your bath.

Most of all, my darling, I want you to know how much I love you, and how much Mommy and Daddy love you. We loved you before you were born and after even more. How bittersweet it was to hold your soft little body in our arms for such a short time-and how hard it was to let you go.

We are trying hard to hold onto the faith that you are home with God's family, happy and safe. I like to think of you cradled in my own dear mother's arms. It comforts me. I can hear her singing softly those old Scottish and Irish lullabies that I heard as a child. I know that she is taking good care of you now and that we will see you again.

None of us will ever forget you. All of us will always love you. You will always be missed.

With love,

Your Nanna

Writing this book has been as painful as it has been therapeutic for me. I find it ironic that the chapter that was the most difficult to write was Maddy's story. I feel such a great need to tell her story over and over, I have mentioned the need to be able to talk about my grandchild several times in this book, and yet when I tried to sit down and actually write about the night she was born I couldn't. I put off even starting the chapter for quite some time and when I finally did start writing I made it as far as being at the Birth Center for the end of Jenn's labor. I was unable to write about the actual birth. I found it hard to even go back and read the little bit I had managed to write. I could talk about it, I had an overwhelming need to talk about it, but I just couldn't write it. I am a very introspective person; that coupled with my education in psychology prompted me to explore my reluctance to write that particular chapter. The most obvious reason is the horrific nature of a stillbirth, especially an unexpected one. I experienced residual effects of the trauma, which I explored in bereavement counseling, and I was reluctant to go back and visit that again. There was certainly a small element of not wanting to let go of her-by making her story public and sharing her with others, on the surface it seemed as though I were giving her up. Perhaps part of this is the fact that I am a very private person by nature; it was not sharing Maddy that was the stumbling block, it was sharing my deepest thoughts and feelings. However, I want to honor her by telling her story and sharing the impact her life and death had on me. This is the ambivalent and contradictory nature of grief. Finally, I decided to make a ritual out of writing her story. I chose a time when I would not be interrupted. I put on music, lit a candle, and placed Maddy's picture and a box of tissues next to my computer. And I wrote.

Ritual can serve many purposes, both religious and secular. Rituals give formality to ceremonies celebrating transitional life events, such as baptism and marriage. Bar mitzvahs and graduation ceremonies are examples of rituals that symbolize life passages. Rituals can honor or memorialize individuals or circumstances. The AIDS memorial quilt is a vivid and potent reminder of the lives lost to the virus. Viewing the quilt makes the epidemic real in a way that seeing statistics in the newspaper can't accomplish. Making the quilt panels to honor a deceased loved one is a healing ritual for many people. According to the Hospice Foundation of America, the use of ritual can be a powerful aid in the grieving process. Rituals performed publicly in a group setting, such as a funeral or memorial service, allow the bereaved to have an identified support system. The public rituals associated with a funeral help to make the death psychologically real; others gather with the bereaved to acknowledge the death, and to validate their grief. Alice Parsons Zulli, in an article on healing rituals written for the Hospice Foundation of America, says "When we experience a break in our emotional, physical or spiritual connections, we naturally seek a new balance point to restore control and harmony with life." She discusses how ritual can strengthen the bonds that connect us, as well as help to restore a sense of balance. Ritual can be done publicly or privately, as a group or individually, making it ideal for families with broad discrepancy in religious beliefs.

Some people find it useful to develop their own rituals. Creating a ritual is not complicated or difficult. A ritual has been defined as any activity that is performed for its symbolic and emotional value rather than its practical value. We wash our hands many times during the day to cleanse them and minimize germs. The Jewish ritual of hand washing after leaving the cemetery or before entering a house of mourning is performed to symbolically wash away the grief. The main difference between a habit and a ritual is the awareness of the meaning the activity holds. The morning routine of fixing lunches and gathering books as part of seeing a child off to school may end with the ritual act of a hug and a kiss. The hug and kiss symbolize that our child is taking our love with them for the day. Lighting a candle, or reading a special poem on the monthly anniversary of the baby's birth date, may be comforting ritual acts. I light the candle I brought home from Maddy's memorial on the 12th of every month at 6:17 pm. If I am away from home, I honor Maddy in a moment of silence. I spend time reflecting on her and on my son and daughter-in-law. Making a donation to a charity can become a ritual act. Many people make a donation to a charity related in some way to a deceased loved one on the anniversary of either the person's birth or death. The charity is chosen with conscious awareness of the meaning it has in relation to the deceased, and it is made on a significant date. My sister loved children and had enjoyed a special relationship as a Big Sister. Over the years I have made many donations to Big Brothers/Big Sisters on her birthday.

The usual rituals associated with holidays can be particularly difficult. Martha Tousley, MS, RN, writes about this in an article called *Getting Through the Holidays.* "Holidays can create feelings of dread and anxiety in those who are bereaved. The cliched images of family togetherness and the often unrealistic expectations of a season filled with picture-perfect, joyful gatherings can cause tremendous stress for those who are *not* grieving, let alone for those in the midst of the painful, isolating experience of loss. Holidays by nature are filled with nostalgia and tradition, but in grief, even the happiest memories can hurt." The very act of decorating my Christmas tree has become an activity that has evolved over the years. I collect Christmas tree ornaments-I try to purchase something each time I travel that is symbolic of the area. Every year as I unpack the ornaments and arrange them on the tree, I reminisce about the trip during which the ornament was acquired. I buy my grandchildren an ornament with the year on it every Christmas. This is a ritual I began with my sons-I purchased an ornament each year that symbolized their interests at that time in their life. I plan on making or purchasing ornaments for Maddy to hang on my tree. Many nonprofit agencies produce holiday ornaments as fundraisers. I have bought at least one ornament every year from AIDS organizations as my way of commemorating the people who have lost their battle with the virus, as well as honoring those who live with HIV. These kinds of ornaments fill a dual purpose, as part of the purchase price goes to the agency selling them. This is important to me, with my strong beliefs in social justice and helping others. Zulli's article states "a ritual is simply a function for getting in touch with that which brings wholeness and meaning." She also says that ritual and celebration affirm an interconnection between our lives and the lives of others. My ornament collection is certainly an affirmation of this interconnection; I have ornaments for my sons, for my grandchildren, to support causes I believe in, and as souvenirs of my travels. As the collection has grown, even the act of decorating the tree has become ritualistic-I light candles, put on music, and pour a glass of wine.

Many families find that incorporating new rituals into their holiday celebrations eases the pain. Rabbi Earl Grollman, in a Hospice Foundation article on holiday memories, writes, "When facing grief and holidays, a powerful use of ritual can be to actually create new rituals, or give oneself the permission to change past rituals that may be too difficult to continue." Ideally, a family should be able to talk together about what will help them to cope with a holiday. There may not be agreement, especially about changing long standing family traditions. Susan Hendricks, who experienced the death of her teenage daughter, has a strong interest in the spiritual dimensions of grief and the ongoing role of ritual in our accommodation to loss. She talks about how she, her husband, and their son have continued some traditions while also creating new ones. "Our holiday rituals have become more centered in the love for each other, and the one who is no longer with us, and are carefully planned taking each one' s need and emotional vulnerability into account." Mary Lou Reed's family goes to the cemetery every Christmas Eve and puts up holiday lights for her grandson Alex. She also ties a big red ribbon around a tree that her family planted near their home.

There are many creative things we can do to remember and honor our grandchild at the holidays. In talking to parents and grandparents I've heard some wonderful ideas of things we can do for ourselves as well as for the community. Some grandparents donate a gift each year that is appropriate for the age their grandchild would be. Kara Jones, in her magazine Different Kind of Parenting (kotapress.com), suggests that if you see an article of clothing you would love to buy for your grandchild, go ahead and buy it, wrap it and put it under the tree. Later the item can be donated to a clothing drive. The MISS Foundation has a wonderful program called the Kindness Project, which started in 1997 as a way for families to honor their deceased child and to help themselves heal. You can order kindness cards from their web site and include one with a donation of food or clothing. Decorate a wreath with ornaments or items that symbolize your grandchild. Hang a stocking and fill it each year with small items that are age appropriate; these items could then be donated to a children's hospital. You could ask each family member to put something in the stocking. This is a nice way for surviving grandchildren, especially siblings, to be able to express their love for the baby. Community centers frequently hold Secret Santa shops for children to purchase or make gifts for family members. You could donate craft supplies or items for purchase. If you shop at a grocery store that gives a free turkey you might want to donate the turkey to a community or social service center with a kindness card attached. The director of a local community center put up a memory Christmas tree and asked members of the community to place an ornament on it commemorating a deceased relative; many support groups do this as well.

Making Memories

One of the things that parents and grandparents struggle with is the lack of memories. There are so few things that we have as memories of the baby. Most of the memories are personal and private ones, such as the parents' memories of feeling the baby move, or listening to the heartbeat during a checkup. There are many ways in which we can make memories to comfort our children and us.

There may be a design or symbol that takes on special meaning for your family. The nursery theme that my son and daughter-in-law chose was a bug pattern. They were going to emphasize butterflies and dragonflies if the baby was a girl. We found ourselves adopting the dragonfly as our symbol of Maddy. This happened almost unconsciously, without actually talking about it. Jenn had a dragonfly charm on a necklace that she had been wearing for awhile. I bought dragonfly charms and chains for my other daughter-in-law and myself. I found a lovely enameled brooch for my mother. Friends who are aware of the special meaning dragonflies have taken on in my life have found many wonderful items with dragonflies and given them to me-these items are so precious to me. I was at a large business meeting out of state about four months after Maddy's birth. A pharmaceutical rep with whom I work commented on my dragonfly necklace. Knowing that she is a very spiritual person who believes in symbols, I shared the meaning of the dragonfly with her. That evening, when I returned to my hotel room after dinner, there was a package on the desk. While at a local pottery place that afternoon, she had seen an item with a dragonfly. The fact that people recognize and acknowledge the symbolism of the dragonfly is evidence of the impact that Maddy's stillbirth has had. I have been amazed at how many things I've found with dragonflies on them. It seems as though everywhere I look I see something. At one point I made a comment to Jenn to please tell me if I was going overboard with the dragonflies. She replied that these were the only things we had and that she loved each and every one. The dragonfly has become a ritual object for our family, something we cherish for its symbolic and emotional value rather than its usefulness. Beryle collects angels for herself and her daughter to commemorate Dakota. "Dakota's birthstone is the aquamarine and anytime I see an angel and especially an angel with his stone, I have to get it. There are Dakota angels everywhere shining their blues."

Sharon Stepleton thinks of her granddaughter Paige as a winter firefly. Paige was born in December. In her devastation over Paige's death, Sharon wrote to her daughter, trying to capture her granddaughter's essence. "Our little Paige was a winter firefly, just like the fireflies you see in July flying over the fields. They light up so brightly then they are gone so quickly. This was our little Paige. She brightened up our days and we had so much hope for her. But just like the fireflies we will never forget her."

Crafts and hobbies are a creative outlet, and they can fulfill our need to do something. On several occasions I have made elaborate scrapbooks for family members to commemorate special events. I had been planning to make a scrapbook for Tim and Jenn after the baby was born. About a month after Maddy died I found myself thinking about the scrapbook more and more, creating it in my mind. I decided that I very much wanted to make it. To my way of thinking, not to make the scrapbook was the same as never mentioning the baby's name or talking about her. I knew I wanted it to be a beautiful acknowledgement of the love and joy surrounding Maddy's anticipated arrival. As I started purchasing the papers and stickers and planning the layout of the pages, I was overcome with sad thoughts of what should have been. I blocked out some weekends to work exclusively on this project, and once I physically started putting the pages together I was surprised at the comfort I derived. It felt good to do something concrete. I did not tell my son or daughter-in-law that I was working on it, instead choosing to give it to Jenn for her birthday. Because it felt so good and gave me comfort, I am also planning on making a scrapbook for myself, using patterned paper and printing out the poems I've written for Maddy.

Photography is another hobby I have always enjoyed. The pictures I took of Maddy are the only ones we will ever have of her, and I have enjoyed using computer programs to make these few pictures appear in as many different ways as possible. I made wallet size photos for everyone who wanted them. I have created fancy frames and designs, and printed these pictures out for myself as well as for my son and daughter-in-law. I also have Maddy's picture out with all my other family pictures. She is my granddaughter and a much-loved member of my family.

There is no reason why you can't make a birth sampler. Don't let anybody tell you that it isn't appropriate-anything that comforts you or your children is appropriate. For some people it is the physical act of needlework or drawing that helps. Many people feel that it is a validation of the baby's life to complete the projects that were planned or begun during the pregnancy. The project may be changed somewhat to become a memorial. I had wanted to make some little quilts for the baby to keep at my house for when I would baby-sit. Instead, my daughter-in-law and I are planning to make a quilt using some of Jenn's maternity clothes, some of the blankets and crib sheets from the baby shower, and a few baby outfits.

Some people need the release of a physical activity to bring them comfort. My mother has one of the most beautiful yards I have ever seen, with gorgeous flowerbeds. She has always enjoyed gardening. When my sister died, she spent hours working in her gardens. The physical act of putting her hands in the soil and digging helped to release some of her pain. She would dig and cry and dig some more. A gardener may plan a remembrance garden, adding a new plant or variety of flower every year. Wilma, whose grandson Jackson was stillborn, planted a memorial garden. Butterflies symbolize Jackson to her family, so she planted a weeping cherry tree because it attracts butterflies. She also planted several flowers around the tree, choosing ones specifically for butterflies. Maddy's maternal grandmother, Kathy, planted a magnolia in her yard when Tim and Jenn became engaged. She planted a tree for Maddy next to the magnolia.

Aside from charitable foundations, there are many ways of making lasting donations in memory of the baby. You can name a star for the baby-there are several internet sites that will send you a chart of the sky and show you the precise location of the star. You can also make a donation to an agency that plants trees on public land. I found a wonderful web site that allows you to pick the state where you want the tree planted. I intend to plant a tree every year on Maddy's birthday, each year in a different state. I was thrilled with the idea of planting a tree, something living, something meaningful, and something that benefits the earth. These concepts all hold meaning for me and I felt certain that my son and daughter-in-law would also appreciate the tree. They received a lovely certificate explaining the tree program, stating that the tree had been donated in memory of Maddy. Many libraries, including school libraries, accept donations of books. You may want to donate an age appropriate book each year in memory of your grandchild. On Mother's or Father's Day you could donate a book in honor of your bereaved child. Nancy, Ethan's grandmother, says "I made a preemie blanket and some preemie booties to give to the hospital on Ethan's birthday and angel date. I went in there acknowledging that the act was not going to heal my heart, or change the fact that Ethan had only lived 24 hours. And in some strange way, giving a gift in Ethan's name, knowing that I would never see him in this life, was very healing."

Make things for yourself as well as for your children. Mary Lou Reed's family put together a tape of special music including a Mozart selection that had been her grandson's favorite since birth. Mary Lou has copied the tape and given it to family members who use it as bedtime music for their babies. Alex's tape helps to keep his memory alive as the family grows. Music has always been an integral part of my life, and on several occasions I've made mix tapes, compiling favorite songs or songs with a common theme. I created a compilation tape for myself that I call Maddy's Mix. The songs in some way relate to Maddy and my feelings during the first few months after her death. Listening to music is a wonderful outlet for every emotion. Many people find music to be an escape. Music has always been a refuge for me, one that can be either soothing or invigorating. The opening notes of a song can immediately transport me to another time and place. In many cases, the lyrics capture the essence of a moment, or a particular rhythm or harmony touches our soul.

Many grandparents feel as though they need to get involved in some way to help prevent the circumstances which led to their grandchild's death, or to help others going through this horrendous experience. You can advocate for more research into miscarriage, stillbirth or neonatal death, as well as for funding to support and increase research efforts. Pat Fife, whose granddaughter Brigid died of SIDS, worked for the Visiting Nurse Association. She established a memorial fund in her granddaughter's name there. The fund helps to support a maternal child program that has SIDS risk reduction as a primary focus. Some grandparents seek out training or utilize their professional expertise to serve as peer counselors. Others may find themselves involved in more public endeavors, such as lobbying for legislation to issue certificates of birth resulting in stillbirth if your state does not already have this legislation. Obtaining a birth certificate is an issue that carries tremendous emotional weight for parents and grandparents. To not issue a birth certificate is a denial that there ever was a life. It saddens and angers us to think that our precious baby's existence has so little meaning. I find it difficult to comprehend how a death certificate can be granted for a person who never officially lived. As Richard Olsen, the Executive Director of the National Stillbirth Society says, "all mothers give birth, it's just that there are different outcomes." When his daughter was stillborn, he searched for an advocacy organization and, finding none, founded the National Stillbirth Society. The goal of this organization is to educate and agitate for greater stillbirth awareness, research funding, and the passage of legislation in every state to recognize our babies' births by requiring states to issue a Certificate of Birth Resulting in Stillbirth. I will never forget the plaintive tone in Jenn's voice as she sat in the rocking chair holding Maddy. She looked up at me and said "So am I a mother or aren't I?" She most definitely is a mother, and a birth certificate would help to authenticate that for her. In May 2004, Arizona, which was the first state to pass the legislation, also passed a bill to provide tax breaks for families with stillborn children.

Each one of us will find a way to memorialize the baby that will help us to cope. Maddy's maternal grandmother had bought many toys throughout Jenn's pregnancy, and during the Christmas season she donated some of them to a charity collecting toys to be distributed to needy children. Jenn's sister, Pam, is extremely creative and talented when it comes to crafts. She had sewn some lovely things for the baby. On what should have been Maddy's first birthday, Pam made a stuffed bunny with the fabric left over from a bunting she had made for Maddy. Some of us may develop private rituals or creative projects. You can join or start a support group. Encourage the local organizations with support groups for bereaved parents to address the unique needs of grandparents by having a separate group. There are a few online support groups specifically for grandparents. Many of the bereavement web sites encourage submissions of poetry or articles if you choose to make a public statement about your grandchild. Just as every person's experience of grief is different, the activities that bring comfort to one person may not be helpful to another. It's important to not only do things that will be meaningful to your bereaved child, but also to you. An analogy I use frequently when I am working with healthcare providers on managing stress, bereavement, and burn out is applicable here. The standard speech made by flight attendants before the plane takes off tells people that in the event of a loss of cabin pressure, oxygen masks will automatically descend. People are advised to secure their own mask before they assist the person in the seat next to them. We cannot help anybody else if we don't take care of ourselves first. Try out different methods of coping until you find what works for you. Don't be afraid to discontinue an activity if it no longer brings you comfort. Once I decided to trust my inner voice about what my strengths and limitations were, I found that I rarely had to consciously search for a coping activity. All of these activities serve as distractions from the free-for-all our emotions engage in. They give us a specific task on which to focus and concentrate. They help to fulfill the need to do something in a situation in which there truly is nothing we can do to change the outcome.

Remember that time by itself will not heal your grief. Many grandparents have said that their greatest moments of peace came when they admitted that this is a grief from which they will not heal. Coping with grief is an active process, and the activities you engage in should be ones that will bring you some degree of comfort. What you do with your time as you search for answers and a way to incorporate this experience does more healing than the mere passage of time.

CHAPTER 6

REDEFINING NORMAL

Grief drives men into habits of serious consideration, sharpens understanding and softens the heart

John Adams

Eventually there does come a time of renewal. Just as the seasonal spring comes with slowly lengthening days and subtly softening and warming air, so does the emotional spring. Gradually, the crying becomes less, and although thoughts of the baby are never far from the surface, our every waking moment isn't guided by grief. We don't awaken sobbing in the middle of every night. We are able to function effectively for longer periods each day. We find ourselves enjoying activities. We once again look forward to tomorrow.

Whether we want them to or not, the days turn into weeks and the weeks accumulate into months. The first anniversary of our grandchild's death comes and goes and we are left wondering what comes next. Nearly all of my energy had gone toward grieving. My task was to survive-to endure the passage of time. I found, as I approached the end of the first year of mourning, that my days became more purposeful. I had a fairly clear picture of what coping mechanisms worked for me. I had given myself permission to feel and fully experience the pain of loss without the confining societal definition of strength. However, I hadn't sorted out my feelings and processed them. Now it was time to think. Time to think and reflect, time to explore the changes I was noticing in myself. Time to acknowledge my areas of ambivalence and attempt to reconcile them with the person I was becoming. I attended a conference for people living with HIV infection, and one of the keynote speakers referred to the mixing bowl of life. When you examine the ingredients in a cake, each one separately doesn't do much, but when mixed together these ingredients turn into a delicious cake. The ingredients, or events in your life, are what make you who you are. I don't want to be defined solely as a bereaved grandmother, but I do need to recognize that Maddy's stillbirth has become a crucial ingredient in the mixing bowl of my life. It has permeated every aspect of my being.

The ideas in this chapter reflect my personal thoughts and feelings on the overreaching concept of a final stage of grief. I have come to believe that there isn't an ending, and in talking to many other bereaved parents and grandparents, I have found nearly universal belief that grief is ongoing. Dr. Kathleen Gilbert states in an online unit called Traumatic Loss and Grief that "grief does not completely end, as some might expect, but will become a part of who that person is, sometimes intense and sometimes existing as a type of 'background noise' in their lives." I personally found no solace in any of the religious cliches, and I found myself avoiding conversations with people who told me that Maddy was in a better place with God. I believe that the best place for a baby is in her parents' arms. I share this part of my journey in the belief that I cannot be the only bereaved person struggling with the concept of a finite and identifiable time for my grief to be over. I am by no means trying to be as prescriptive as the various models and theories I've discussed. My granddaughter's life, albeit too brief, was significant. My hopes and dreams were shattered, many of my deepest held beliefs and assumptions challenged, but my love for her remains intact.

Much of the literature on grief calls this time resolution or even recovery. The stages model refers to resolution as the final stage. The word resolution and the concept of the final stage of grief imply a definite ending. Once you have accomplished this, your grief is supposedly over and done with. Margo says "I don't feel any resolution. I know this is life. That none of us are guaranteed all the things we want or need. That loss is as much a part of life as birth. But I'm not resolved to losing Peyton, and I don't think I ever will be." I have chosen instead to use the word renewal. I struggled for quite some time over the concept of recovery-how could I possibly recover from Maddy's stillbirth? At the same time that I was angry because society expected me to get over her death, I also felt guilty because I couldn't seem to meet those expectations. As the months passed and I read many books on loss and grief, I spent a great deal of time thinking about my personal beliefs. A pamphlet given to me by Sister Dolores, a Franciscan nun who has been a very special person in my life for many years, captured how I felt. The pamphlet talks about the loss of a baby and it says that one of the tasks of grief is letting go. It then goes on to say that what the bereaved is letting go of is the pain, not the memory of the baby. Maddy will always be a part of my life. By acknowledging that I will never resolve her death, I am able to explore how to renew living in a world that doesn't include her physical presence.

The concept of renewal as opposed to resolution did not come quickly or easily. Many months of counseling, reading, and thinking passed. In the beginning, as I eagerly devoured books on grief, it helped to read about the emotional roller coaster. I could identify with that, and it helped to know that I wasn't alone. As the months went by I revisited my grief books; I had reached a point where I was functioning effectively more often than not, yet inside, I felt no better. The sections on recovery contained little that reflected my thoughts and feelings. Friends expressed surprise when they asked how I was doing and I answered truthfully that I was not doing well, so I started saying I was fine. I expressed concern to the therapist I was seeing that I didn't seem to be healing, and even though she said that I was being too hard on myself, I still felt as though I must be doing something wrong. Eventually I discontinued therapy, mistakenly believing that my lack of closure indicated a shortcoming on my part. I went back and studied theories of grief, certain that I had missed a key point. Unfortunately, everything I read only increased my sense of isolation and inadequacy.

During this time of introspection, I noticed that my journal entries were changing. I also realized that instead of drawing comfort from what I was reading about grief, I was experiencing increased frustration. I bought book after book, hoping I would find one that expressed what I was feeling. I had put off writing this chapter because I had no idea how to write about recovery and closure. When

I finally permitted my writing to give voice to my thoughts without intellectual editing, I realized that I could not write about acceptance, recovery and closure as traditionally defined by psychotherapists. I can accept that Maddy did not survive delivery, but I will never accept that there was a reason or purpose to this. I have changed direction in my quest for meaning-there is no meaning to be found in terms of a reason for Maddy's death. There is, however, much meaning to be discovered in my decision to once again actively participate in living. There is also meaning in my refusal to accept that Maddy's death erases her existence. Alice Parsons Zulli writes for Hospice Foundation of America "Bereaved people often have a strong desire to maintain their attachment and relationship with the deceased loved one, while society often demands rapid closure." If closure means moving on and leaving the memory of Maddy behind, then I will never have closure. Maddy is a very significant part of me, and I will carry her along for the rest of my life journey. She resides within my heart, and as such will never be "gotten over." Maddy's death cannot be resolved, nor can my grief over the void in my family. To resolve, to let go, to move on, means denying my family history. Not only does that diminish Maddy, it diminishes my sense of who I am and my place in the world. Lorraine Ash, whose daughter Victoria was stillborn after a healthy full term pregnancy, says that closure is not something she seeks, as that would end her relationship with her daughter.

It was while these thoughts were being clarified that I came across the writings of Donnali Fifield. She is a twin who after significant, multiple, traumatic losses, including the death of prematurely born twin sons, came to the realization that there would be no recovery or closure. She has written a book about her experiences with and thoughts on loss and bereavement. She openly challenges the professional community to look at and rethink the concept that grief can be neatly packaged, dealt with, and resolved. I developed an e-mail acquaintance with her that sustains me as I write that it is perfectly normal to search for a continued connection with my granddaughter. It is neither pathological nor dysfunctional to think about her, to miss her, and to talk about her. Donnali states that one of the reasons she wrote *William & Wendell: A Family Remembered*, is to challenge the theory of resolution. In the first chapter, she says "The advice to get over grief hurts, I think, because it denigrates the reality of a loss. Being told how to feel silenced my emotions. Even more painful, it dismissed my losses. If I was supposed to get over the deaths quickly, then the deaths themselves must not deserve much notice."

Once I started thinking of the word renewal and all its implications, I felt a sense of calm. I was able to cease my internal struggle over our society's perception that death is something to be gotten over. I could invest my energy in discovering not only how to incorporate the stillbirth experience into my being, but also the life lessons. I could actively look for ways to honor and memorialize Maddy. She has no visible presence in this world, but I do. My thoughts, my actions, and my words can ensure that she will not be forgotten. I am able to explore and appreciate things in a new way. I no longer believe in coincidence. As I mentioned previously, I was not supposed to be present at Maddy's birth, but I was meant to be there. I found Donnali at a time when I desperately needed a connection with somebody who had navigated the convoluted path of loss, and had given prior voice to what I was feeling.

Despite my determination to appreciate each and every day and to be open to symbolism regarding Maddy, one event in particular challenged something I said at her memorial. I had made the comment that when I felt a snowflake on my cheek I would know it was Maddy telling me it was time to stop crying. I delivered those remarks on November 22. I live in the Mid-Atlantic region of the East Coast. We usually get snow late in the winter, if at all, and rarely is there significant accumulation. On Friday December 5 it started snowing and when it stopped on Saturday, the amount recorded near my home was eight inches. Although winter is not my favorite season, I love the first snow. I get as excited as a small child waiting to see if school will be cancelled. When snow is forecast, I am the one running to the window every few minutes to see if it has started. As I stood in my front yard lifting my face to the snowflakes, I remembered my comment. The snow was lovely as it drifted and swirled around me, brushing my face and landing on my cheek. I laughed through my tears at the irony of a major snowfall this early in the season. And I shook my fist at the sky, knowing I was not ready to stop crying.

At first I was bitter and resentful every time I purchased something with a dragonfly. I didn't want symbols of Maddy-I wanted my granddaughter. I wanted to be buying things for her, not things to remind me of her. Initially, I wanted to buy every dragonfly item I saw. As time passed I became more selective; just as I would not have purchased every single toy or article of clothing for Maddy, I now look for items I would have wanted even without a dragonfly. I collect Native American pueblo pottery. I contacted the gallery owner I deal exclusively with, telling her about Maddy and asking her to keep an eye out for a pot with dragonflies on it. She remembered an artist who had done dragonfly designs in the past and contacted him to locate a pot. I've turned the search for dragonfly items into a meaningful activity, and the things I've acquired have a personal story and connection beyond the significance of the dragonfly. I wear my necklace almost every day, and I find myself touching the dragonfly frequently. It has become a ritual object for me. I am thrilled rather than saddened when friends give me a dragonfly-it lets me know that they are thinking not only of me but also of Maddy. The concentric circles of lives she has touched spread ever wider.

My grief journey has by no means been a direct road from loss to renewal. Many of the detours have been like taking a wrong turn when driving late at night. You sense that you are headed the wrong way, but you are reluctant to turn around. You keep telling yourself that your destination is just a bit further. I forced myself to socialize before I really wanted to. I listened to others who told me it would do me good to get out and be with people, and I didn't possess the emotional strength to stand up for myself. I went on vacation unconsciously expecting to leave my grief at home. I believed that healing occurred when my life was back to normal, not realizing that normal would need to be redefined. Margo defines healing as learning to live with the loss. "Yes, life will return to a new normal. Normal now is to go forth, to honor Peyton every day by remembering him and how much we loved him for nine months. Normal is to not let this grief eat us up. To continue with our lives. To try to help others if we can. Normal is getting through one day at a time."

Nancy, Ethan's grandmother, states:

> I decided that I would participate in the March of Dimes Walk America as a way to bring closure. I raised $125 and participated in the walk. But after it was over I still felt the same. After careful evaluation of my feelings, I have come to accept the fact that there will never be complete closure in this life. I have had to surrender to the fact that my first grandchild died and left a hole in my heart. For some strange reason, the knowledge that I won't ever completely heal has brought me acceptance and has made it possible to deal with my loss. This hole in my heart is part of my new identity. I will forever be a bereaved grandparent.

A noticeable turning point for me occurred at the time when I least expected anything positive to happen. As the first anniversary of Maddy's birth approached, my anxiety level started to rise. I found myself crying again every day as I drove to work. I noticed that I was withdrawing somewhat. My sleep patterns became severely disrupted. I dreaded November 12. I couldn't imagine a way to endure the day that should have been her first birthday. I had arranged months earlier to be off work that day. The morning of November 12 was a chilly, rainy, dreary start to what I anticipated to be an extremely bleak day. It had begun to rain during the night. My thoughts were that the weather suited my mood perfectly. I made a pot of coffee and lit a scented candle. I curled up on the sofa with some books and my journal. Most of the morning was spent thinking about Tim and Jenn and Maddy. I read for a while and I wrote in my journal. I had purchased two cloisonne dragonflies on a business trip many months prior, intending to give one to Tim and Jenn on Maddy's birthday. For some reason I had left the one I bought for myself in the box. I opened it ceremoniously and hung it around the taper I had from Maddy's memorial service. The candle was on my mantle with two framed pictures of Maddy behind it. I placed another taper with a silk butterfly for Jackson, Wilma's grandson, next to Maddy's candle. Most of the day was rather uneventful. I cried often, but the tears were calm, not the raging torrent I had expected. I read and relaxed and looked at her pictures. As the afternoon moved toward evening, I directed my thoughts to the ways in which I felt changed by Maddy's death. I concentrated on thinking about making peace with the pain rather than being consumed by it. I had spent the past year fighting the pain and the grief, and I was exhausted, both mentally and physically. I started redefining normal as it pertains to my life. I talked out loud to Maddy, telling her how very much I wanted her and how loved she is. I had certainly not anticipated any sense of peace on this day, but at times that is what I felt. Overall, the day was calm and quiet. The comfortable scent of coffee and candles filled my home. I chose to honor Maddy by showing her the love and comfort in her family. At exactly one minute after midnight I declared "I did it, I have survived this first of many birthdays." Interestingly enough, the rain, which had started shortly after midnight the night before, didn't stop until after midnight the day of Maddy's birthday- the same amount of time from when Jenn first started having labor contractions to when Maddy was delivered. The following morning dawned with a magnificent sunrise, and the sun shone brilliantly all day. The autumn leaves stood out in a final, defiant burst of color.

One of the lessons I've taken to heart is that none of us are promised tomorrow. I've made more time for family and friends, and I've redefined inconvenience. I had begun this shift in attitude after my sister's death, but the stresses and pressures of raising two sons overcame my determination to stop putting things off until tomorrow. Five months after Maddy's stillbirth, my mother spent the week of her birthday visiting my brother in Colorado. When I heard that they were going to Salt Lake City for a long weekend, I immediately made arrangements to take the time off, book a flight and make hotel reservations, and join my family. This was done without my mother's knowledge. The look on her face when I walked into her hotel room and the joy she and I shared during those days was well worth any so called inconvenience. My closest girlfriend and I have talked for years about a getaway weekend, but the conversation never progressed beyond the daydreaming stage. Work and family demands always seemed to get in the way. We finally made a hotel reservation and a commitment to each other that we would actually follow through on our plans, and we spent a wonderful weekend together. Pat Fife spoke at her granddaughter's memorial service. She spoke of Brigid's gift as one of time. "Her short life taught me that I had to appreciate and enjoy every minute of it because you never know when you might not have it." Pat's husband worked at the World Trade Center for thirty-two years. 9/11 occurred nine months after their granddaughter's death, and that tragedy made them all the more aware of Brigid's gift of time. Her husband travels a great deal with his job, and Pat knew she needed to restructure her life so they could have time together. She was able to resign from her job, and she now travels with her husband.

I am indeed a different person than I was before November 12 2003, but most of my changes are not visible. Many of these changes are positive ones. I've thought about what meant the most to me in the first few days after Maddy died, and I was surprised at the things I remember. I was emotionally numb, too paralyzed to reach out to anyone. The people who called and came to my house without being asked are the ones I remember the most fondly. The friends who were able to sit silently with me for extended periods of time, unafraid to confront grief and witness my pain, will always have a special place in my heart. The casual business acquaintances that came up to me when I returned to work and told me how sorry they were stand out in my mind. I do not hesitate to offer a simple statement such as "I'm so sorry" to someone who has experienced a loss. I used to be hesitant to bring it up if I didn't know the person well. Now I know how much those simple affirmations mean when you have been bereaved. I am more assertive in calling or taking food to a bereaved friend; I used to ask if there was anything I could do, tell my friend to call if they needed anything, and leave it at that. I send cards after the funeral because I know how empty and lonely those days are.

I take advantage of opportunities to educate people about bereavement and grief. When a friend shared with me that one of his close friends had just experienced the death of his daughter, he said he didn't want to intrude, that he would call them in a few days. I urged him to call immediately. I told him that newly bereaved people are frequently unable to reach out and that we need our friends to come to us. I ran into a family friend at the grocery store who told me that the reason she hadn't called for several months was that she didn't want to make things worse by reminding my son of his loss. Did she really believe that a day goes by when my son and daughter-in-law aren't thinking of Maddy? I told her that the absolutely worst thing that could ever happen had already occurred, and that nothing she could say or do could possibly make it worse. I then suggested that perhaps her silence, which in effect negated Maddy, was worse than the tears she might provoke by remembering the baby. Yet again, I find myself in a position of advocacy. Ours is not only a death denying society, but also a death fearing one. People are afraid to talk openly about death and grief; bereaved persons are made to feel as though outward expressions of grief are a weakness. Reluctance to hear us talk about the death of loved ones perpetuates the isolation in which grieving people exist.

I've changed my gift giving habits. Instead of buying something, I prefer to do something special with the people who mean the most to me. I took my grandson to Colorado for a week for his tenth birthday. The experience of flying in an airplane, exploring the Rocky Mountains, and spending concentrated, quality time together provided memories that will last a lifetime. Anything I could have purchased would have been long since discarded, but we talk about our trip often. I like to think that along with all the fun we had, my grandson got to know who he is and where he comes from a little better. That is the kind of gift I want to be known for giving-the gift of belonging to something bigger, the legacy of love and family.

To say that the experience of losing a grandchild has made me a better person is too simplistic. Although I have been profoundly changed by the stillbirth of my granddaughter, in many ways the change is more of a transformation. The primal pain I feel acts like a toxic agent, stripping away the defensive layers that have built up over the years. The values and beliefs that were formed during my teenage years have been strengthened. I am better able to resist the lure of commercialism, and to distinguish between need and want. I am committed to giving more of myself to my family. I make a conscious effort to live by my values rather than just stating them. I am determined that my grandchildren will grow up knowing who I am and what I believe in. I want them to know that they matter, that every minute I spend with them is precious and that they are loved unconditionally. I would rather give them a sense of the magnificence the world holds than a closet full of toys. The expression of awe on my grandson's face when he gazed at the view from an overlook in Rocky Mountain National Park is seared forever in my heart. I'd like to think that for the rest of his life he would be able to recall his tenth birthday present from me, whereas I can guarantee that he couldn't say what I gave him for his ninth.

Many of my personality traits have become stronger. I've always been introspective, but now I actually make time for quiet reflection and thought. I try to allow myself time to re- energize without feeling guilty about whatever household chore isn't being accomplished. I am by no means an isolationist, but my natural tendency toward being a loner has increased. I have never minded being alone, or doing things by myself, and I notice that many of my most peaceful hours have been those spent in my own company. Perhaps that's because I don't feel as though I have to pretend with myself. If I feel like crying, I can do so without fear of being judged. I find that I tend to withdraw somewhat in casual social situations. I censor my comments about Maddy because of a concern that people are tired of listening to me. I am more tentative about relationships. I have never been an insecure person, but my inner sense of security has been shaken, and I feel emotionally vulnerable. I have more of a need for reassurance; I no longer take anybody's continued love or support for granted. The other side of this is that some of my close friendships have deepened. I communicate with my friends on a more intimate level than before. Susan Hendricks says "We are no longer the same people we used to be: our personalities have undergone significant shifts as we deal with our loss. Our values and what we find meaningful are no longer what they were. Time and life have become precious commodities: we find we cannot abide idle chit-chat or meaningless socializing."

I have always cherished and embraced life as a precious commodity, but I never had quite the respect for time that I do now. I refuse to feel guilty over spending the afternoon curled up with a book. I am nourishing my soul. I am making a concerted effort to take advantage of unexpected opportunities and not agonize and rationalize. I'm learning to be more spontaneous and flexible about schedules and to-do lists. My dirty kitchen floor will still be there tomorrow but the friend who wants to meet for dinner tonight might not. I am aware that one's entire being can change drastically in a split second. Vacations used to be packed full, with every moment of every day accounted for. I would study where I was traveling in advance and prepare a sightseeing itinerary. My intended schedule was frequently unreasonable, causing frustration when it couldn't be completed. I've learned that unexpected changes or disruptions caused by weather can actually lead to new adventures. Visiting an attraction on a chilly rainy day is an opportunity to explore leisurely without crowds or lines. Allowing enough flexibility in the schedule to just relax has opened a new world to me. I used to view any time not spent sightseeing as wasted time; I now realize the importance of taking time, whether it is at home or while on vacation, to replenish.

I am aware of a greatly decreased tolerance for idle conversation. Time has taken on new meaning for me, and I don't have time to chat with no purpose other than to fill the conversation. Some friendships have fallen by the wayside due to a lack of understanding and acceptance of my grief. At first I felt guilty and worried that I should make more of an effort, but then I gradually came to the realization that I had no interest in prolonging superficial acquaintances. The friendships that weathered the unpredictable storm of my grief have become richer and fuller.

I'm still not good at asking for help. I don't readily admit, even to close friends, how much I still hurt and how hard it is sometimes to get through the day.

Journal entry:
> I feel as though I'm living in 2 worlds. When I talk to my hospice friends or any of my online acquaintances through the bereavement web sites, I feel normal and validated. There is nothing wrong with crying or wanting Maddy. But the rest of the world, the world I have to function in on a daily basis, seems to believe that it was a singular event which is over and done with. I feel like I'm living 2 lives, an outward one in which I interact and function and appear as I did before, and an inner one in which I keep a major secret from everybody. Yes, I still hurt. Yes, I still cry. And no, there isn't a day goes by that I don't think of and long for Maddy.

I am working at being as kind and loving to myself as I am toward others. Part of this is realizing my limits and learning to be more assertive about them. My colleague Pat teaches CPR for healthcare professionals several times a year. I have frequently accompanied her, and I would demonstrate and observe return demonstrations of infant CPR while she demonstrated on the adult dummy. There is absolutely no way I can do this now. I realize I cannot place myself in situations such as this. The next step is accepting that this self-awareness is a sign of strength rather than weakness.

My lifelong love affair with words has been reignited. All through my adolescence and early adulthood I wrote, filling notebook after notebook. I wrote poems about my love for my infant sons. I wrote down the bedtime stories I made up. As my time filled with the multitude of activities surrounding my children, I wrote less and less. Much of my professional experience has involved writing, but for many years I did little creative writing. When my life came to an abrupt standstill I needed an outlet for the love and pain and despair, and I turned again to the solace provided by words. I read and devoured the writings of others, and I started writing poetry again. There are days when the words flow as freely as my tears. Although I think of my writing as my gift to Maddy, the reality is that Maddy has given me the gift of reconnecting with myself. I am returning to the creative activities I valued and put aside.

Friends have commented that I seem to worry less. I know that I feel less anxiety about life situations. In thinking about an explanation for this, the most obvious one is that the absolute worst thing that could ever happen to me has already happened. At this point, everything else pales in comparison. I don't worry about everyday occurrences as much as I used to because I have concrete knowledge that worrying will not change anything. I am able to do a quick mental triage, and for the most part have greatly decreased needless worrying. Perhaps part of this comes from a deliberate attempt to cope by living and dealing with each day as it comes, rather than fretting about what awaits me tomorrow. I have always been someone who was organized and detail oriented; I lived by my to-do lists. This illusion of control was abruptly wrenched from me when Maddy, whose very existence was carefully planned and prepared for, was born still. It took many months for a glimmer of empowerment to surface; relinquishing the perception of control allows me the freedom to appreciate things for how they truly are, rather than constantly trying to make them into something else. I am more able to live in the here and now and savor each moment as it happens, realizing that exact moment will never come again.

My emotions seem to be right on the surface. This has been particularly difficult for me because I have always been an emotionally private person, not readily sharing my feelings even with those closest to me. Never having been much of a crier, I am amazed at how easily the tears come now. I took my granddaughter to see the play Scrooge and cried during the scene where Scrooge sees Tiny Tim's gravestone. I still find it difficult to look at babies and toddler girls. I skip over the pages in store ads that feature toddler girls. If I'm with friends who are exclaiming over a cute child in a restaurant I tear up. I have always considered myself empathetic, but I seem to feel things now on a much deeper, almost visceral, level.

My earliest thoughts and journal entries saw my grief journey as a path distinctly separate from the rest of my life. As I explored my feelings about resolution, and decided to adopt the word renewal instead, I realized that my grief journey is part of my life journey. Viewing it as a distinctly separate path is too limiting and furthers the sense of isolation. If I am to incorporate Maddy's stillbirth into my life, I must also incorporate my journey. One of the activities I enjoy when I go to Colorado is hiking. I have favorite areas and trails. Most of the general areas have several different trails-they all start from the same point and eventually they all end up back at the same point. Some of the trails are easy, fairly level hikes. Others are strenuous, involving climbing and increased altitude. My grief journey is a trail branching off but not completely separate from my life journey. The grief trail will cross over the life trail in many places. It often runs parallel to the life trail. Hiking my grief trail will always bring me back to my life trail. I am trying to approach my grief journey in the same manner in which I hike. If I only have a few hours before my flight home, I'll hike a quick easy trail. I would never hike a long, difficult trail without water and sun block. Those are the things I take along to protect me. I can try to protect myself emotionally by surrounding myself with people who accept the fact that my grief journey is going to be a lengthy, unpredictable hike. I can use meditation and visualization techniques as coping methods when emotions threaten to overwhelm me at a time when I can't give in to them. I can let myself experience the sorrow and pain when I have time for a more strenuous hike through my grief. I try to respect my emotions on my grief journey the same as I respect my body on a hike. If the elevation leaves me short of breath, I'll stop and rest. If I need a few minutes alone, I give myself permission to close the door to my office or not answer the phone at home.

Hiking a steep trail that ascends in altitude is never easy. My chest hurts and my calves ache. I stop to catch my breath and consider turning back. But I continue upward, and when I reach the top, the view is so glorious that the discomfort ebbs. I'm still climbing the mountain of my grief journey. I'm starting to realize that there is no top to this mountain. I'm learning to make peace with the pain and keep on climbing. Just as I stop frequently on the trail to admire the view, so do I appreciate the beauty in my daily surroundings. I am not alone on this journey. Maddy is with me constantly, residing in my heart and drawing my attention to the wonders of nature. I take delight in every sunrise and sunset. I pay particular attention to the moment just before day slips into evening, when the colors in the sky deepen until they seem to slide off the horizon. I am astonished by the brilliance of the stars in the velvety black night sky. Did they always sparkle this brightly, or is the effect enhanced when seen through the prism of my tears? Maddy leads me every step of the way, showing me that life is indeed beautiful and worth living. She has taught me a vital life lesson- the ultimate beauty is not found in the destination of the journey, but the scenery along the way. I don't want to miss a single sunrise or sunset. I want to see every sparkling star and constellation. My brother may be mildly annoyed, but I will make him stop at every scenic overlook as we drive through the Rockies. And I will continue to run outside at the first snowfall and feel Maddy kissing away my tears. There are still many times when those are tears of pain, but there are also times when my eyes fill with an overflow of love. My heart will always contain the joy and excitement and love I felt for the nine months of Maddy's existence. She is part of me, the daughter of my youngest son. I will forever be her grandmother.

Oh Maddy, how I love you.

CHAPTER 7

MEANINGFUL COINCIDENCE

She was no longer wrestling with the grief, but could sit down with it as a lasting companion and make it a sharer in her thoughts.
Middlemarch
George Eliot (Mary Ann Evans)

Much of my time since Maddy's stillbirth has been spent thinking about what it means to be spiritual. I have never thought of myself as a religious person, yet I have always had a strong sense of spirituality, without really giving much thought to what that means. I think that much of what is considered coincidence is not nearly as accidental as it appears. Several times during my grief journey I've read back through the books I purchased in the first anguished weeks after Maddy died. A few stand out as beacons of support in the bleak wilderness that is grief. *Life Touches Life* is Lorraine Ash's eloquent account of her journey through grief after the stillbirth of her daughter, Victoria Helen. I have returned to this book several times, and each time I read it I discover more common ground. One of the many areas Lorraine covers is the belief that she maintains a connection with her daughter. I struggled with this silently for far too long. My mind discounted what my heart knew to be true. I argued with myself. I finally stopped the internal dialogue and listened to my heart.

I had several experiences that, as a spiritual person, I could not discount. More than one of these involved Pat's Aunt Helen. Pat and I are good friends as well as co-workers. We have shared several significant and traumatic life experiences, and there is a strong connection between us. Aunt Helen died on Maddy's due date, a mere five days after her stillbirth. That in itself was significant to both of us. I was completely empty, with no emotional reserves available to comfort Pat. I felt terrible, as she had done so much for me; now she needed comfort and I had none to give. I opened the newspaper on the second day Maddy's obituary ran, and what I saw so stunned me that I stood up and walked away, then came back to make sure I had really seen it. I immediately called Pat and asked if she had seen the paper yet-she replied no, and I told her that I couldn't describe what was there but that she had to look at the obituary page immediately. Aunt Helen's obituary was positioned directly under Maddy's. Maddy's last name begins with an H and Aunt Helen's name begins with a W- in an effort to make everything fit, obituaries are sometimes printed out of alphabetical order. There were two full pages of obituaries that day, so it took on a high degree of significance that those two were positioned together, with Maddy's being on top. My reaction was that Maddy wasn't alone, that Aunt Helen, who dearly loved babies and had never had one of her own, was holding her. People with a stronger religious leaning commented either that Aunt Helen, being older, was showing Maddy the way, or that Maddy, having died first, was welcoming Aunt Helen to heaven. Pat took the two obituaries and had them mounted on green card stock and laminated-they were the perfect size for a bookmark.

The next event occurred a few months later. Pat was in the process of cleaning out her aunt's house. The house backs up to parkland. There was one window in particular that Aunt Helen used to gaze out; she had seen a red fox many times from that window. As Pat stood by the window reminiscing, she noticed a perfectly preserved dragonfly on the windowsill. She carefully placed it in a box lined with cotton and gave it to me. Just days after, I was driving home one evening at dusk and a red fox ran across the road directly in front of my car. I live in a housing development, so this was unusual.

The two symbols of the people we dearly loved, seen so close together, had to have deep meaning. And yet, I kept telling myself this wasn't possible. After all, I am "only" Maddy's grandmother. I questioned why I was seeing dragonfly designs everywhere I looked. I wondered if dragonflies have been popular for a long time and I've just never noticed them. When I talked to Pat about this, she assured me that she believes Maddy is there, with me always. She feels that whether dragonfly items have been popular all along or whether this is something new isn't really important-what is important is that I am finding them. I am actually drawn to them. Rarely do I have to actively search for a dragonfly item-they seem to present themselves to me. Pat has been with me as I've walked into a little shop where the first item in the display case or window is a piece of jewelry with a dragonfly design. They are the symbol that Maddy's spirit is with me. They are Maddy's way of urging me to keep living. It wasn't until I finally stopped intellectualizing and questioning the possibility of a spiritual connection with Maddy that I was able to accept the warm certainty of her presence.

Very tentatively, I started asking others if they felt any type of spiritual connection to dead family members. I was nervous that I would be accused of being in denial over the fact of Maddy's death. I spoke to a few friends I felt comfortable with, and was encouraged by their belief that Maddy is with me. At the same time, I read the September/October 2004 issue of the MISSing Angels newsletter, which contained an article by Joanne Cacciatore-Garard that left me exhilarated. Joanne is the founder of the MISS Foundation. Her article captures everything I was thinking. With Joanne's permission, I am reprinting the entire article, as it truly does address this issue beautifully.

Wonderment
By Joanne Cacciatore-Garard

I've spent my entire life in a sense of wonderment-a sort of tug-of-war-with faith. Many questions about life, and death, danced around inside my head as early as I can remember, and no adult seemed to adequately quench my thirst for an answer. When Cheyenne died, I was in my mid-20's. By that point in my life, I had given up the quest to find a Creator. I acquiesced to the logic of Darwinian thought; that is, until I watched as they lowered the pink satin casket into the ground.

I wondered if this was really the end. I wondered if I would ever see my little girl again and I went looking for answers again. I asked for signs. I pleaded for some morsel of hope that one day I would be reunited with my child, taken far too soon.

The answers came for me. At first, they were subtle. I questioned them-I analyzed them away. Rationalization is a powerful defense mechanism. So the answers became more conspicuous. So apparent, in fact, that much of the content of my first book, Dear Cheyenne, focused on the "miracles", or as Jung called them, "meaningful coincidences" that I had experienced since her death. Still, the battle between faith and doubt persisted. And I wondered.

Ten years of wonderment later, I found myself in the midst of a tenuous year. This year was the 10th anniversary of Chey's death. Ten years gone; an entire decade. My emotional tumult began on July 27, 2004 and didn't let up until mid-August. Finally, when I was able to regain some stability in my decade-gone-grief experience, Elisabeth, one of my best friends and my mentor, died. Oh, I knew she wasn't well. In fact, I had a dream one month prior to her death that she died. I was as prepared as I could have been to say goodbye to someone so incredibly important in my life.

And then, I began to wonder. Chey died in July of 1994. I was living in north central Phoenix at the time. We chose the first funeral home and mortuary that answered the phone. At the very same time, in the summer of 1994, Elisabeth moved to Arizona and was planning her own funeral-she pre-purchased her services at the same funeral home in south Scottsdale and the same cemetery in north Scottsdale that I had chosen for Chey. Was it coincidence? I wondered. As I endured the four days of her funeral services, memories of

Chey's death flooded my thoughts. I wondered if Chey would be one who greeted her when she died. Then, I wondered if there really was a life after death at all. And the wondering thoughts continued to plague me until Sunday, the final day of Elisabeth's services.

Exhausted, I came home and cried most of the afternoon. My head hurt and my heart ached. I missed my daughter, my mom, and my friend (grief certainly is cumulative). Around 11:00 p.m., I went onto the front patio and sat in my rocking chair outside. I leaned my head back and was "talking" to Elisabeth in my head (one time, when Elisabeth was on Oprah, she told her that she would send her closest friends signs after she died...she told Oprah that she'd "pinch her tush"...) I had tears rolling down the sides of my face and I closed my eyes. I asked her if she was with Chey now and if she was okay. I told her that I was one friend, due to my enduring tug-of-war, that would need a very clear sign. So, I silently said...a shooting star, Elisabeth. Send me a shooting star. I opened my eyes and immediately saw a very bright shooting star flying from the east to the west sky. I shook my head and laughed. I suppose that in a few months, given my proclivity to doubtfulness, I'll wonder about whether or not I imagined the star...or whether it was just a coincidental, astronomical fluke. But for now, I'm thankful for the miracle that I received that day and for the reassurance that my little girl found Elisabeth. They are both in good hands.

And I've come away from this, not with an unshakable faith. I'm not sure that is something I can ever acquire. But I do have wonder. And wonderment is a good thing, I've learned. Wonder leads to discovery, and discovery leads to awakenings. And, as I've learned and experienced, awakenings lead to miracles. In the end, faith wins every time.

Reading this article has given me the courage to explore more openly the significance of symbolism and an ongoing connection with Maddy. It certainly is a meaningful coincidence that this particular issue of the newsletter contained the very thoughts that had been tumbling around in my mind. I was stunned to read somebody giving voice to the beliefs and contradictions and confusion that I feel. Carl Jung, a Swiss psychotherapist, observed coincidences that were connected in such a meaningful way that their occurrence seemed to defy the calculations of probability. He used the term synchronicity to describe this phenomenon. Too many seemingly improbable things have happened in connection with Maddy for me to shrug them off as mere coincidence. The above article was published at the same time that I was tentatively coming to terms with the belief that Maddy is with me. However, the timing of Joanne's article goes even deeper-it appeared as the first anniversary of Maddy's stillbirth approached. Just as I needed to read many grief books and hear others voice the same emotions that I was feeling right after Maddy died, so did I need to read these public words of wonderment at this particular time in my journey

I have always enjoyed traveling, and one of the many things that attracted me to my current job was the travel associated with the position. For most of the year after Maddy died, I traveled for work reluctantly, finding for the first time in my life that I just didn't want to be away from home. And yet, it is on my trips out of town that I most frequently find dragonfly items. Perhaps Maddy is trying to tell me that she is always with me, that I am not leaving her behind when I travel. Perhaps the message goes even deeper-maybe Maddy is showing me that if I am able to believe in a spiritual connection, then I will find her everywhere. These dragonflies are to me what the shooting star was for Joanne.

I re-read Lorraine Ash's book, *Life Touches Life*, turning to it often in those hours deep in the night when sleep eluded me, always finding wisdom and insight. "I chose to accept her presence without further questioning," she says. "There was more joy in that decision and more warmth, too. That decision continues to bring me peace and allows me to deepen my relationship with my blessed daughter."

Other grandmothers have indicated that they also feel their grandchild's presence in their life. Beryle took a job with a day care center after her grandson's stillbirth. She felt a special connection to two little boys in her classroom, and she is sure that Kota's spirit was what drew her to these children. She enjoys riding in motorcycle rallies, and feels strongly that Kota rides along with her. Margo takes pinwheels to Peyton's gravesite on a regular basis. She says "The first time I did this (and many times since then), as long as I am talking to Peyton, the pin wheels spin around like crazy. When I am quiet, they slow way down or stop altogether for a while. I have a very strong feeling that Peyton loves when I come to "visit" him and that he likes me to talk to him." She also shared that when her daughter was having a difficult labor with Peyton's little brother, she and her daughter both felt Peyton's presence reassuring them.

Pat Fife shares the following experience, which occurred about six months after her granddaughter's death. "My husband and I had to attend a black tie fund raising function. I was feeling rather down and just saw it as another thing to get through. However, as I dressed for the affair a sort of light appeared in my mind. I remembered that one of the prizes at this event was a trip to Hawaii. Something told me that I would win this trip. I did. I felt that angel Brigid had arranged this. It was her way of telling me that I needed to be happy again. One morning in Hawaii I awakened early. I looked out our door and saw the most spectacular double rainbow. I knew our angel had arranged that." Pat says she has seen Brigid rainbows in Ireland, Scotland, Spain, Quebec and Key West. She saw one at Thanksgiving on the way to her sister's home.

John Cox and his wife Cheryl share that their best connection with their grandson A.J. is a white butterfly. John says "Often, when we are feeling particularly sad or overwhelmed a small white butterfly will appear. It may be the wrong season for butterflies or an unusual place to see them, but our butterfly somehow shows up. Cheryl and I have sat in our back yard, feeling lonely on a gray fall day, long after butterflies should be gone to the season, only to see a white butterfly dance along the fence, stop to say 'hello', and then dart over the fence and out of sight." A butterfly is also the symbol for Mary Lou Reed that her grandson Alex is with her. She lives in a part of the country where roses bloom almost all year long, and she often brings in a rose for Alex to sit on her kitchen counter.

I made a wall hanging for the Birth Center for Maddy's birthday-every aspect of that wall hanging was significant. It was important to me that the wall hanging be personal and symbolic, yet cheerful. Tim and Jenn delivered Maddy in the yellow room so the fabric with the dragonflies was yellow. I chose a bright print that looked like something you would see in a baby's nursery. I spent many evenings with the fabric spread out on the floor, looking through pattern books, trying to get some inspiration for what design to use. I wanted something large enough to showcase the dragonflies on the fabric. I thought about Maddy while contemplating the fabric, and one evening my creative energy kicked in and I knew exactly what I wanted to make. I cut the dragonfly print fabric in the shape of a large heart to symbolize Maddy's heartbeat, and appliqued it to a square of background fabric that matched one of the colors of the dragonflies. I used a bright pink for the outer border as the stereotypical symbol of a girl. I quilted around the outside of the heart so it would stand out. The day before Maddy's birthday I stopped at the Birth Center after work to drop off the wall hanging. As I stood on the sidewalk locking my car, I realized that I had parked in almost exactly the same spot as on the night Maddy was born, and walking up to the entrance, I was uneasy. As soon as I entered, I knew it was right for me to be there. The staff ushered me in the back office so we could chat. I gave them the wall hanging and they asked if I would like to go upstairs to the yellow room. I didn't hesitate, it never occurred to me not to go, yet if I had been given time to think about it I never would have wanted to see that room again. Somehow, it simply felt right that we should gather in the room that one year ago had been the scene of mind numbing shock and trauma. We sat in the birthing room with the wall hanging and decided where it should hang. We talked about Tim and Jenn and Maddy. The room was bright and peaceful, the atmosphere soothing and homey, a marked contrast to the last time I had been there. The room was quite noticeably warm, so I took my jacket off. I was still warm, and the realization came to me that the warmth I was feeling was Maddy's presence. The room was filled with her on that chilly November afternoon.

The most consistently meaningful coincidences have occurred with my grief soul mate, Wilma. Wilma and I found each other through an online support group for bereaved grandparents. We discovered that our precious grandchildren had been delivered on the same day and began communicating directly with one another. Butterflies symbolize her grandson to Wilma, and dragonflies symbolize my granddaughter. Butterflies and dragonflies are frequently found together in nature. They are drawn to the same flowers and environment. The connection has continued to deepen as we've shared increasingly personal thoughts and feelings. We both are very spiritual although not particularly religious. We were hesitant as we disclosed to one another our sense that our grandchildren are together, and that Maddy and Jackson are the force that brought us together. We both struggled with letting go of the intellectual debate raging in the logical part of our brain and listening to what our hearts declared to be true. Wilma was the first grandmother I discussed this with, and it was so affirming to find that she felt the same as I did. We were in very close touch during the week leading to what should have been our grandchildren's first birthday. Wilma told me that she planned to release balloons for Jackson and Maddy. When she described what happened with the balloon release, I laughed and cried at the same time.

Everyone took the time to write special messages for our little angels. We then went outside to Jackson's tree, tied the messages to the balloons, and set the balloons free to sail up. Of course, plans cannot always go smoothly. My neighbors have a very big tree with very big branches. Two of the biggest balloons never made it past that tree. They were still there when we came inside for the evening. At first it made me sad...then I started smiling. A butterfly balloon and a Snoopy balloon holding a heart that says "I love you" were the two balloons that stayed with us.

These were the balloons that looked the most like something a child would love. Our two grandchildren, two children's balloons…coincidence?

I received this e-mail and my immediate thought was the same as Wilma's-the symbolism of our grandchildren telling us they were still with us. The next day I got a second e-mail from her.

The balloons that were caught in my neighbor's tree were still there in the morning. Just after noon we noticed that the butterfly had broken loose and sailed away. There was no way that the Snoopy balloon could go….it was really tangled in the branches…so we thought. Just a few minutes later, Snoopy caught the wind and sailed after the butterfly. It seemed to me that Maddy and Jackson were staying close by until their birth/angel day had passed. Then, today, saying good-bye and sailing off together.

I went to Tucson two months after my granddaughter was born still. I saw dragonfly items everywhere and purchased several, signing the credit card slips with my tears each and every time. The pain was raw and fresh, a searing dagger through my heart, the wound still open with no protective scab to cover it. Even though I pounced eagerly each time I saw an item with a dragonfly, I was bitter and resentful because I wanted to be buying little t-shirts. Almost exactly one year later I was in Belize. I thought about Maddy constantly, and cried more than I had for a while. The day before I left I went up into the Mayan mountains to see the waterfalls. There was nobody else at the first two falls. I stood in a little clearing gazing at the falls, drawing in the sharp, clean air of the mountains. I stood quietly, trying to absorb some of the tranquility surrounding me, as if by osmosis I could take it home. A dragonfly darted in front of me, pausing and dipping as though willing me to look. It circled around and when it passed before me again there was a butterfly with it. High in the Mayan mountains, thousands of miles and many cultural centuries from home, Maddy was there with Jackson. In a life defined for me by her absence, she makes her presence known.

John and Cheryl have also had the experience of their grandson joining other deceased children. "Once, while traveling, we stopped in a lovely city park that held a memorial to two teenagers of that town who had died in separate car accidents. As we read the memorial plaques, three white butterflies floated by. Pausing just long enough to be seen and appreciated, they flew up and over the trees. A.J., we thought, had brought his two new friends with him."

I had two significant experiences as the second Christmas after Maddy's death approached. I purchase ornaments for my grandchildren every year. I was out of town the weekend of the craft show where I usually select their ornaments, so I went to a Christmas shop at a local nursery. The shop was filled with artificial trees, each one lavishly decorated in a theme. I found ornaments relating to the activities my grandchildren were involved in. As I made a final inspection of the decorations, I noticed a tree with butterfly ornaments. On closer inspection, I found a large sequined dragonfly. It looked like something I would expect to see in New Orleans for Mardi Gras. The dragonfly was certainly not a traditional ornament, nor was it my usual style. I purchased it without hesitation, having no idea how I was going to use it. When my tree was up, I looped the dragonfly over the bare branch sticking straight out of the top, and it was a perfect tree topper. Two weeks later I took my daughter-in-law to an off Broadway production as her Christmas present. The playhouse is located in a wonderful hotel, and on the ground floor are several prestigious shops. We arrived early enough to browse. We wandered into a jewelry store with elegant window displays of cut glass. Jenn and I were examining the glass pieces when we were drawn to a shelf with small hand blown glass figurines. As we exclaimed over the lovely items we noticed several dragonflies on the next shelf. Each one was different and we chose ours with great difficulty. The clerk, sensing that the dragonflies symbolized something very special, wrapped them beautifully in silver boxes.

There came a point where I had to stop questioning. I needed to end the struggle with the logical, rational part of me and open myself to accept the signs of a continued connection with Maddy. I'm not sure why it was so hard for me to believe that all of the supposed coincidences weren't really coincidences. Maybe I was scared. Scared to trust and believe and suffer yet another loss. Scared that friends would think I had finally tumbled off the narrow ledge of sanity. I want to believe that my sister Blair, who died before fulfilling her dream of having a child, is looking after Maddy. I can't explain how or why, but I do know that I feel Maddy's sweet presence. She sends dragonflies my way as a reminder that life is precious. She has brought new friends into my life, people I most likely would never have met without the initial connecting thread of grief. She is everywhere. She is in the wild flowers growing with abandon in my back yard, delighting all who sit on my patio in the summer. She is in the clean sweet scent of freshly mown grass. Her reflection glows back at me from the highly polished pueblo pottery made in the way of the elders with clay dug by hand from the earth. The cool clear water of a mountain stream carries her along as it moves lazily across stones worn smooth by time. I see her in the endless cycle of day to night, as the sky flares with the final intense colors of the sunset. The gentle spring breezes whisper her name. She is in the joyous song of the birds at dawn, eager to awaken me. So I will stop attempting to rationalize and I will listen to my heart. There is certainly a pervading sense of absence when my family gathers, the knowledge that two core members, my sister and my granddaughter, are not physically with us. However, as I mentioned in my remarks at Maddy's memorial service, my family does not count its members by those sitting at the dinner table. Maddy is with me. My tears may lessen over time, but they will never completely dry, nor will they be forgotten.

And I believe.

BIBLIOGRAPHY

Ash, Lorraine. *Life Touches Life A Mother's Story of Stillbirth and Healing.* Troutdale, Oregon: NewSage Press, 2004

Berman, Michael, M.D. *Parenthood Lost Healing the Pain After Miscarriage, Stillbirth, and Infant Death.* Westport, CT.: Bergin & Garvey, 2001

Borg, Susan and Lasker, Judith. *When Pregnancy Fails.* Boston, Mass.: Beacon Press, 1981

Covington, Sharon N. *Silent Birth When Your Baby Dies.* Minneapolis: Fairview Press, 1986, revised 2003.

Davis, Deborah L. *Empty Cradle, Broken Heart: Surviving the Death of Your Baby.* Golden, CO.: Fulcrum, 1991.

Davis, Kellie. *Forever Silent Forever Changed The Loss of a Baby in Miscarriage, Stillbirth, Early Infancy* New Jersey: booklocker.com, Inc. 2001.

Doka, Kenneth J. *Living with Grief: After Sudden Loss.* Bristol. PA: Taylor & Francis, 1996

Fifield, Donnali. *William & Wendell: A Family Remembered.* San Francisco CA: Times Two Publishing Company, 2000.

Galinsky, Nadine. *When A Grandchild Dies: What to Do, What to Say, How to Cope.* Houston, Texas: Gal In Sky Publishing Company, 1999

Gerner, Margaret H. *For Bereaved Grandparents.* Omaha NE: Centering Corporation, 1990.

Golden, Thomas R. *Swallowed by a Snake: The Gift of the Masculine Side of Healing.* MD: Golden Healing Publishing LLC, 2000.

Heavilin, Marilyn Willett. *Roses in December.* Eugene, Oregon: Harvest House Publishers, 1987.

Kennell, Marshall and Klaus, John. *Maternal-Infant Bonding.* St. Louis: The C.V. Mosby Company, 1982.

Kitzinger, Sheila. *Education and Counseling for Childbirth.* New York: Schocken Books, 1977.

Kohner, Nancy and Henley, Alix. *When a Baby Dies The Experience of Late Miscarriage, Stillbirth and Neonatal Death.* New York: Routledge, 2001.

Lewis, C. S. *A Grief Observed.* New York: HarperCollins Publishers, Inc., 2001 edition Originally published 1961

Lothrop, Hannah. *Help, Comfort & Hope after Losing Your Baby in Pregnancy or the First Year.* Fisher Books, 1997

Powning, Beth. *Shadow Child An Apprenticeship in Love and Loss.* New York: Carroll & Graff Publishers, Inc., 2000

Rando, Therese. *On Treating Those Bereaved by Sudden, Unanticipated Death.* In Session Psychotherapy in Practice, Vol. 2, No 4, pp59-71 John Wiley & Sons, Inc., 1996

Reed, Mary Lou. *Grandparents Cry Twice: Help for Bereaved Grandparents.* Amityville, New York: Baywood Publishing Company, Inc., 2000

Ryan, Adrienne. *A Silent Love: Personal Stories of Coming to Terms with Miscarriage.* New York: Marlowe & Company, 2000.

Schiff, Harriet Sarnoff. *The Bereaved Parent.* New York: Crown Publishers, 1977.

INTERNET RESOURCES

ADEC Association for Death Education and Counseling
An international interdisciplinary organization committed to furthering understanding of grief and bereavement. The Forum, newsletter-Jan/Feb/March 2003, Volume 29, Issue 1 Professional Development theme: Grandparent Grief, *Grandparent Grief: "Nipped in the Bud"* by Tom Easthope, CDE; *Grandparent's Grief-Who is Listening?* by Mary Lou Reed, RN, MA
April/May/June 2004, Volume 30, Issue 2 Professional Development theme: Perinatal Loss
http://www.adec.org

AGAST   Alliance of Grandparents, A Support in Tragedy, International
Bereavement packet, many fact sheets and articles, newsletter, discussion forums-an active grandparents support forum
http://www.agast.org

American Pregnancy Association Stillbirth: Surviving Emotionally
http://www.americanpregnancy.org

Bereaved Parents of the USA
http://www.bereavedparentsusa.org

Centering Corporation   For Bereaved Grandparents- booklet by Margaret Gerner
Education & resources for the bereaved-many booklets on grief available **Grief Digest**, a quarterly magazine containing articles from many well-known grief experts
http://www.centering.org

Center for Loss & Life Transition   bookstore, newsletter, articles
Dr. Alan Wolfelt, Director, is an internationally known grief educator,
author and grief counselor
http://www.centerforloss.com

Compassionate Friends   Stillbirth, Miscarriage and Infant Death,
The Grief of Grandparents
http://www.compassionatefriends.org

Crisis, Grief & Healing   web site of Tom Golden, LCSW, a
psychotherapist who specializes in healing from loss. Good attention
given to men and gender differences. Many articles and a discussion
group
http://www.webhealing.com

First Candle/ SIDS Alliance   nonprofit health organization working
to increase public participation and support in the fight against infant
mortality, 24 hour bilingual crisis counselors available 1-800-221-
7437   booklet - Surviving the Death of a Baby
http://www.sidsalliance.org

Grief Healing   Getting Through the Holidays   web site of Marty
Tousley, RN, MS, CS, CT. Marty is a psychiatric nurse and certified
bereavement counselor who has written several articles and booklets
on loss and grief.
Marty welcomes e-mail: tousleym@aol.com
http://www.griefhealing.com

Grief in a Family Context   web class, Kathleen Gilbert, PhD.,
C.F.L.E., C.T.   Department of Applied Health Science, Indiana
University
http://www.indiana.edu/~famlygrf

Grief Reactions Associated with Stillbirth and the Death of a
Newborn Baby
http://www.grieflink.asn.au/baby.html

Grief Watch   resources for bereaved families & professional caregivers
http://www.griefwatch.com

Helping After Neonatal Death   For the Family and Friends of Parents Who Have Lost a Baby- Advice for the Holidays   many other articles
http://www.handonline.org

Honored Babies   web site with several support groups, including one for Grandmothers
http://www.honoredbabies.org

Hospice Foundation of America   numerous articles on loss and grief, annual bereavement tele conference information and transcripts, e-newsletter
http://www.hospicefoundation.org

International Stillbirth Alliance   a coalition working to promote stillbirth research, education and awareness
http://www.stillbirthalliance.org

KotaPress   Founded in 1999 by Kara and Hawk Jones after the stillbirth of their son, Dakota, as an alternative safe space for grief writing. Accepts poetry submissions. Online magazine for bereaved parents-Different Kind of Parenting, Loss Journal
http://www.kotapress.com

March of Dimes   Stillbirth fact sheet, The Double Sorrow of the Grandparents, bereavement packet mailed on request
http://www.marchofdimes.com

McDonald, Julie.   Parental Grief Following Pregnancy Loss: The Influence of Social Support   postgraduate study submitted to the School of Psychological Science, La Trobe University, Victoria, Australia. October 2003

M.I.S.S. Foundation non-profit international organization offering online support; discussion forums include one for grandparents; newsletter, articles, place to submit poetry and memorials, Kindness Project, annual conference
http://www.missfoundation.org

National Mental Health Association Coping with Loss-Bereavement and Grief, How to Deal with Grief
http://www.nmha.org/infoctr

National Stillbirth Society articles and activism specifically for stillbirth, goal of passing legislation in every state to issue a "Certificate of Birth Resulting in Stillbirth"
http://www.stillnomore.org

SHARE Pregnancy & Infant Loss Support
http://nationalshareoffice.com

Sudden Infant Death Syndrome Alliance
http://www.sidsalliance.org

Some Facts Psychologists Know About...GRIEF
http://www.psc.uc.edu/sh/SH_Grief.htm

Still Birth & How to Survive Pregnancy Loss
http://borntoosoon.freeservers.com

Stillbirth: Unexpected Heartbreak by Ann Douglas
http://www.thelaboroflove.com

The Lasting Trauma of Stillbirth by Mark Moran, MPH
http://my.webmd.com

Willowgreen Grief Tips by Jim Miller
http://www.willowgreen.com

Wisconsin Stillbirth Service Program- WiSSP   When Your Baby is Stillborn, Ten Common Myths About Children and Grief
http://www.wisc.edu/wissp